The Elizabethan Translations of Seneca's Tragedies

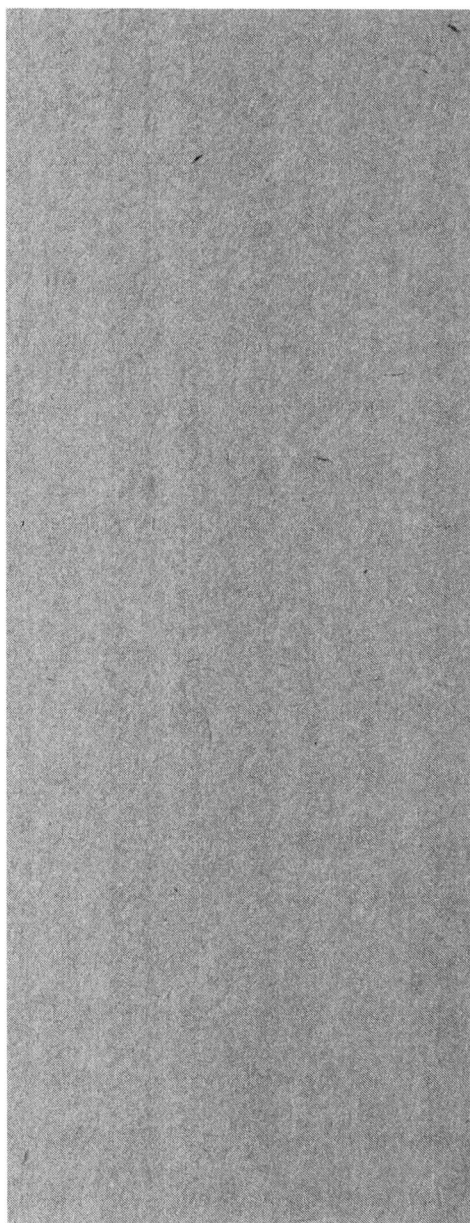

THE

ELIZABETHAN TRANSLATIONS

OF

SENECA'S TRAGEDIES

E. M. SPEARING

Fellow of Newnham College, Cambridge

CAMBRIDGE:

W. HEFFER & SONS LTD.

1912

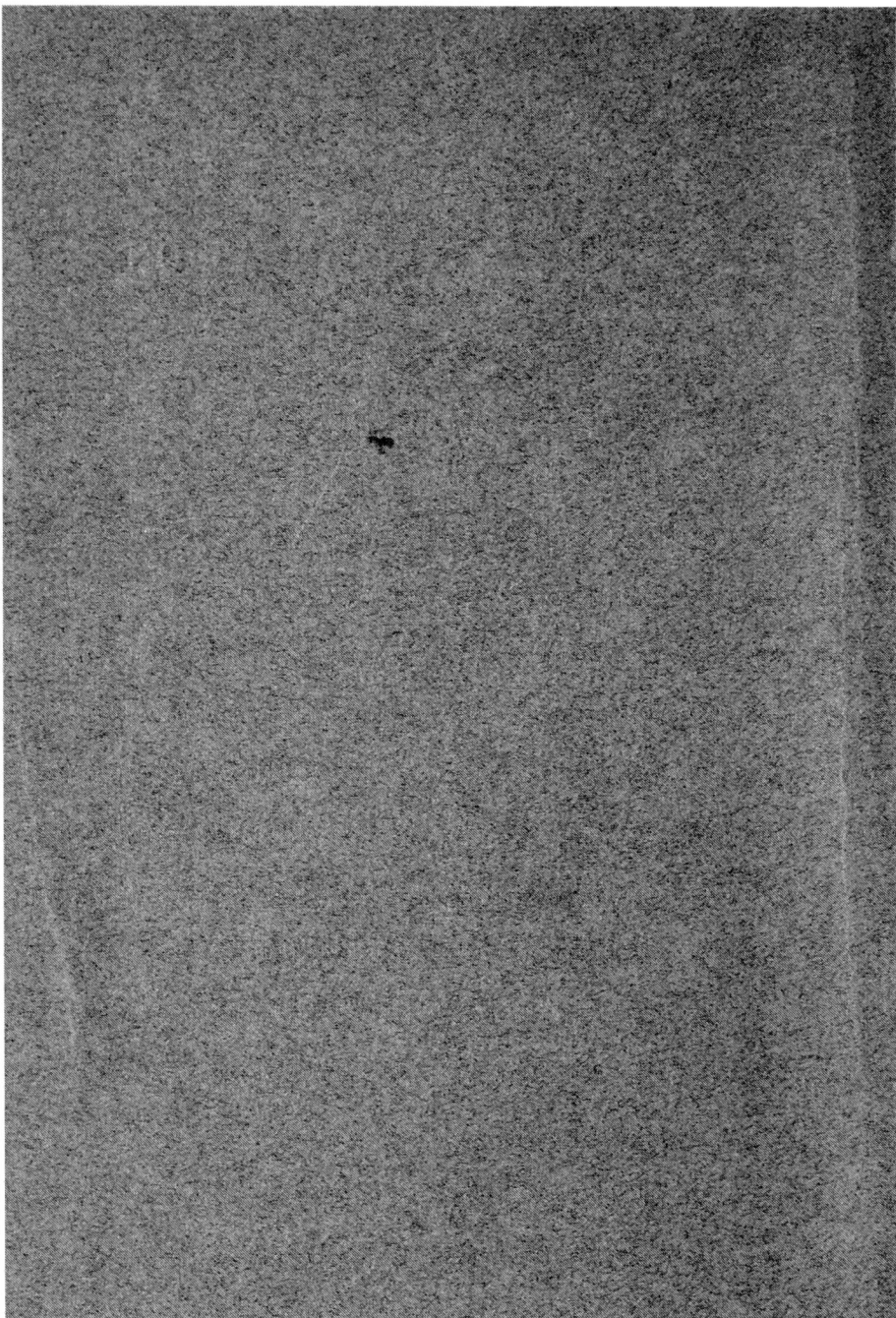

ELIZABETHAN TRANSLATIONS OF

SENECA'S TRAGEDIES

LONDON AGENTS

SIMPKIN, MARSHALL, & CO., LTD.

THE
LIZABETHAN TRANSLATIONS
OF
SENECA'S TRAGEDIES

E. M. SPEARING

Fellow of Newnham College, Cambridge

CAMBRIDGE
W. HEFFER & SONS LTD.
1912

PRINTED BY
W. HEFFER AND SONS LTD
104 HILLS ROAD, CAMBRIDGE

CONTENTS

ERRATA.

p. 11, line 1, for *wrough* read *wrought*.

p 52, ,, 23, for *vy* read *vp*.

p. 71, ,, 7, for *fauours* [? *sauours*] read *sauours*

p 73, ,, 30, for *hoci* read *hoei*.

p. 75, ,, 3, for *N E* read *M.E.*

, *Hercules*

e Tragedies.

255323

CONTENTS

Introduction.

INTRODUCTION

So much attention has been directed of recent years to the influence of Seneca's tragedies on the Elizabethan drama by such works as Fischer's *Kunstentwicklung der englischen Tragödie* and Cunliffe's *Influence of Seneca on Elizabethan Tragedy*, that it is somewhat surprising that the Elizabethan translations of Seneca have remained in comparative neglect.

One of the reasons for this neglect has doubtless been the difficulty of access to the original editions and the lack of any satisfactory modern reprint. The first editions of the separate translations are extremely rare, and in some cases only one copy— that in the British Museum—is known to exist. The 1581 edition of the collected plays is also scarce. At present only one modern edition exists, and that not an altogether trustworthy one, *viz.* the Spenser Society's reprint (1887) of the edition of 1581. This is now out of print, and can only be obtained with difficulty. Professor W. Bang, of Louvain, has, however, announced that a reprint of the first editions of the translations by Jasper Heywood and John Studley will shortly appear in his series *Materialien zur Kunde des älteren englischen Dramas*, and this should do much to facilitate the study of these plays.

This difficulty in consulting the original editions has rendered most of the work done on the subject very unsatisfactory. Thus the Spenser Society were content merely to reprint, as an introduction to their edition, Warton's account of the translations in his *History of English Poetry*, now more than a hundred years old. The articles on the various translators in the *Dictionary of National Biography* contain much valuable information, but are not always reliable. Thus the article on Studley states that no copy of the original edition of his *Medea* is extant, whereas one is to be found in the British Museum, and that on Nuce gives 1561 as the date both of Studley's *Agamemnon* and Nuce's *Octavia*, though the former was certainly, and the latter probably, produced in 1566.

In 1909 there appeared a German dissertation on the subject, *Die englischen Seneca-Uebersetzer des 16. Jahrhunderts*, by E. Jockers, Ph.D. Strassburg. It treats very fully the relation of the separate translations to their original, and contains a careful analysis of the peculiarities of style of the five translators, but its value is lessened by its failure to discriminate between the early editions and the *Tenne Tragedies* of 1581. This mistake is not of great importance in the case of Heywood, Studley, and Nuce, since the 1581 edition is practically a reprint of the earlier editions, though even in their case collation with the original text would have removed certain difficulties which confronted Dr. Jockers.[1] In the case of Neville's *Œdipus*, however, this mistake vitiates the whole of Dr. Jockers' treatment, as the text of 1581 differs in almost every line from that of 1563.

Dr. Jockers' account of the lives of the translators and the dates of their work is also untrustworthy,

---

[1] *e.g.* on pp. 84, 85, Jockers expends several lines in proposing the emendation *Phebe* for *Thebe* (*Ag., Tenne Trag.*, f. 146, l. 23), the reading which actually occurs in the edition of 1566.

and shows too much reliance on the authority of Warton, and of the *Dictionary of National Biography*.[1] Moreover, the value of his quotations from the *Tenne Tragedies* of 1581 is considerably lessened by the misprints which occur on almost every page.[2]

The greater part of the material in this volume had been collected before Dr. Jockers' dissertation appeared, and after reading the latter I felt that there was still room for another treatise on the subject which should pursue a somewhat different line of treatment, and should be based on a careful study, not of a reprint, but of the original editions. At the same time I wish to acknowledge gratefully the help which Dr. Jockers has afforded to all future students of the translations by his exhaustive treatment of their relation to the Latin originals.

My best thanks are due to Professor P. G. Thomas, of Bedford College, London, to whose kindness I am greatly indebted, and to Miss M. Steele Smith, of Newnham College, Cambridge, who first brought the subject before my notice. I owe much to the unfailing kindness of Dr. W. W. Greg, of Trinity College, Cambridge, who generously lent me his copy of the 1581 edition, and has given me valuable help and advice. I wish also to take this opportunity of thanking Dr. J. N. Keynes, Registrary of the University of Cambridge; Mr. Aldis Wright, Vice-Master of

---

[1] *e.g.* on p. 77 he repeats the incorrect assertion of the *D N B.* that no copy is extant of the 1566 edition of Studley's *Medea.* Again on p 76 he states "John Studley wurde um das Jahr 1545 geboren In der Schule von Westminster erzogen, trat er mit ungefahr 16 Jahren in das Trinity College in Cambridge ein," though the Register of Cambridge University shows that Studley matriculated 12 May, 1563.

[2] *e g* on pp 93, 94, the following misprints occur in quotations from the *Tenne Tragedies* —*Glance* for *Glaucc* (p 93, l. 5), *te* for *the* (1 9), *trancling* for *traucling* (l. 27), *did* for *stack* (p. 94, l. 8), *spayse* for *payse* (1 31), *craning* for *cramming* (l. 33).

Trinity College, Cambridge; Dr. Henry Bradley, of Oxford, and others who have helped me in my investigations.

My thanks are due also to the Syndics of the Cambridge University Press for permission to republish certain paragraphs of my article on this subject which appeared in the *Modern Language Review* for July 1909; and to Professor W. Bang, of Louvain, for permission to use material forming part of the introduction which I have prepared for the reprint of Studley's translations in his *Materialien*.

NOTE.

The system of reference employed throughout this volume is a double one When separate editions of the translations exist, reference is made both to the first edition and to the *Tenne Tragedies*, the source from which the exact words of the quotation are taken being mentioned first. All variants of any importance in the other text are inserted in square brackets. Owing to the lack of foliation or pagination in several of the separate editions, reference is made in their case to the signature References to the *Tenne Tragedies* are to the folio and line. When no separate edition is extant, the reference to the *Tenne Tragedies* is preceded by the title of the play, unless this has already been made clear by the context.

I.

SENECA'S TRAGEDIES AND THE ELIZABETHAN DRAMA.

In the sixteenth century the popularity of Seneca's tragedies was immense. To English dramatists, struggling to impose form and order on the shapeless, though vigorous, native drama, Seneca seemed to offer an admirable model. His tragedies contained abundance of melodrama to suit the popular taste, whilst his sententious philosophy and moral maxims appealed to the more learned, and all was arranged in a clear-cut form, of which the principle of construction was easy to grasp. The great Greek tragedians were little studied by the Elizabethans. Greek was still unfamiliar to a large number of students; and it may be doubted whether in any case Æschylus or Sophocles would have been appreciated by the Elizabethan public. The Senecan drama, crude and melodramatic as it seems to us, appealed far more strongly to the robust Englishmen of the sixteenth century, whose animal instincts were as yet only half subdued by civilization.

The importance of the influence exercised by Senecan tragedy upon the development of the Elizabethan drama is now generally admitted. The extent of this influence has been demonstrated by J. W. Cunliffe in his *Influence of Seneca on Elizabethan Tragedy*, and by R. Fischer in *Kunstentwicklung der englischen Tragödie*. It affected both the substance and the form of the drama. The division into five acts, and the introduction of the Chorus, as in *Gorboduc, The Misfortunes of Arthur*, and *Catiline*, may be taken as examples of the influence of Seneca on the form of the Elizabethan drama, whilst in regard to matter and treatment Senecan influence was yet more important. It was seen in the treatment of the supernatural, in the selection of horrible and sensational themes, in the tendency to insert long rhetorical and descriptive passages, in the use of stichomythia, in the introduction of moralising commonplaces, and in the spirit of philosophic fatalism.

Under these circumstances it was but natural that students who read Seneca's tragedies with delight, and had perhaps taken part in the performances which were frequently given in the colleges of their own University,[1] should wish to make him known to their less learned fellow countrymen, and to win fame for themselves by translating into the best English verse at their command an author who seemed to them so well fitted both to please and to instruct. Thus one of the translators states that it was at the "ernest requeste" of "certaine familiar frendes" that he had "thus rashly attempted so great an enterprise," and continues:

---

[1] Professor G. C. Moore Smith in his article *Plays performed in Cambridge Colleges before 1585* in *Fasciculus J. W. Clark dicatus*, pp. 267—270, states that though the records of Cambridge Colleges are most imperfect during the early part of Elizabeth's reign, he has been able to ascertain that *Troas* was acted at Trinity College in 1551-2, and again in 1560-1, *Œdipus* in 1559-60, and *Medea* in 1560-1, and that *Medea* was also acted at Queens' in 1563.

They . . . willed me not to hyde and kepe to my selfe that small talent which god hath lente vnto me to serue my countrey withall, but rather to applye it to the vse of suche yonge Studentes as therby myght take some commoditie.[1]

During the reign of Elizabeth all the ten tragedies then ascribed to Seneca were translated into English verse. Three of these—*Troas*, *Thyestes*, and *Hercules Furens*—were translated by Jasper Heywood, younger son of John Heywood the epigrammatist, and fellow of All Souls' College, Oxford. Alexander Neville, a Cambridge student and a friend of George Gascoigne, translated *Œdipus*. John Studley, scholar and fellow of Trinity College, Cambridge, was responsible for the versions of *Agamemnon*, *Medea*, *Hercules Œtæus*,[2] and *Hippolytus*. Thomas Nuce, fellow of Pembroke Hall, Cambridge, translated *Octavia*; and the remaining play, or rather fragments of two plays, *Thebais*, or as it is sometimes called *Phœnissæ*, was rendered into English by Thomas Newton, who had been a student at both Oxford and Cambridge.

To Heywood belongs the credit of being the pioneer in this work. His *Troas* was published in an octavo edition in 1559, and his *Thyestes*, also in octavo, in 1560. His *Hercules Furens* appeared in octavo in 1561. Neville's *Œdipus* was written, so he tells us, in his sixteenth year, *i.e.* in 1560, but it was not published till 1563, when it appeared in octavo· Nuce's version of *Octavia* is in quarto; it is undated, but there is an entry which probably refers to it in the Stationers' Register for the year July 1566—July 1567. Studley's *Agamemnon* appeared in octavo in 1566,

---

[1] John Studley. *Agamemnon.* (1566.) Preface to the Reader [omitted in the *Tenne Tragedies.*] See also the passage quoted *infra*, p. 27, from Neville's dedicatory epistle to Dr. Wotton.

[2] The Bodleian Library contains a fragment of an unpublished translation of *Hercules Œtæus* which is attributed to Queen Elizabeth.

3

and his *Medea,* also in octavo, later in the same
year. No separate editions are extant of his *Hercules
Œtæus* and *Hippolytus,* but two entries in the
Stationers' Register for the year 1566-7 make it
probable that these two translations appeared in
quick succession to *Agamemnon* and *Medea.* In 1581
Thomas Newton collected all these versions of separate plays, and published them, together with his
own *Thebais,* added to make the edition complete
in a quarto volume entitled " Seneca His Tenne
Tragedies. Translated into Englysh."

Contemporary references show us that the translations were widely read and highly esteemed. Some
lines by a certain T. B., prefixed to Studley's version
of *Agamemnon* (published 1566) indicate that Heywood's *Troas* had enjoyed striking success—a success
which apparently exceeded its merits in T. B.'s
estimation.[1]

When *Heiwood.* did in perfect verse,
    and dolfull tune set out,
And by hys smouth and fyled style
    declared had aboute,
What roughe reproche the Troyans of
    the hardy Grekes receyued,
When they of towne, of goods, and lyues
    togyther were depryued.
How wel did then hys freindes requite
    his trauayle and hys paine,
When vnto hym they haue [?gaue] as due
    ten thousand thankes agayne?
What greater prayse might *Virgill* get?
    what more renoume then this,
Could haue ben gyuen unto hym,
    for wrytyng verse of hys?
Did *Virgill* ought request but thys,
    in labouryng to excell?

---

[1] Some allowance must be made for the fact that Heywood
was an Oxford man, whilst Studley and his friends belonged to
Cambridge.

Or what did fame gyue to him more,
    then prayse to beare the bell ?
May *Heywood* this [thus ?] alone get prayse,
    and *Phaer* be cleane forgott
Whose verse & style doth far surmount
    and gotten hath the lot ?
Or may not *Googe* haue parte with hym,
    whose tranayle and whose payne,
Whose verse also is full as good,
    or better of the twaine ?
A *Neuyle* also one there is,
    in verse that gyues no place
To *Heiwood* (though he be full good)
    in vsyng of his grace.
Nor *Goldinge* can haue lesse renome,
    whych *Ouid* dyd translate :
And by the thondryng of hys verse
    hath set in chayre of state.
With him also (as semeth me)
    our *Edwardes* may compare,
Who nothing gyuyng place to hym
    doth syt in egall chayre.
A great sorte more I recken myght,
    with *Heiwood* to compare,
And this our Aucthor one of them
    to compte I will not spare.
Whose paynes is egall with the rest
    in thys he hath begun,
And lesser prayse deseructh not
    then *Heiwoods* worke hath done.

Ascham in his attack on rime in the *Scholemaster*
(published 1570, but written before 1568) includes the
translators of "Ouide, Palingenius, and Seneca"
together with "Chauser, Th. Norton of Bristow, my
L. of Surrey, M. Wiat, Th. Phaer" as examples of
writers who "have gonne as farre to their great
praise as the copie they followed could cary them,"
and considers that "if soch good wittes and forward
diligence had bene directed to follow the best
examples, and not haue bene caryed by tyme and
custome to content themselues with that barbarous
and rude Ryming, emonges their other worthy

praises, which they haue iustly deserued, this had not bene the least, to be counted emonges men of learning and skill more like vnto the Grecians than vnto the Gothians in handling of their verse." [1]

William Webbe in his *Discourse of English Poetrie* (1586), mentions "the laudable Authors of Seneca in English," and Francis Meres in *Palladis Tamia* (1598) says "these versifiers for their learned translations are of good note among us, Phaer for Virgils Æneads, Golding for Ovid's Metamorphosis . . . . the translators of Senecaes Tragedies."

Nash's well-known passage in his preface "To the Gentlemen Students of both Universities" prefixed to Greene's *Menaphon* (published 1589) is worth quoting in this connection :—

It is a common practise now a daies amongst a sort of shifting companions, that runne through every arte and thrive by none, to leave the trade of *Noverint*, whereto they were borne, and busie themselves with the indevors of Art, that could scarcely latinize their necke-verse if they should have neede, yet English *Seneca* read by candle light yeeldes manie good sentences, as *Bloud is a begger*, and so foorth, and, if you intreate him faire in a frostie morning, he will affoord you whole Hamlets, I should say handfulls of tragical speaches But O griefe! *tempus edax rerum*, what's that will last alwaies? The sea exhaled by droppes will in continuance be drie, and *Seneca* let bloud line by line and page by page at length must needes die to our stage which makes his famisht followers to imitate the Kidde in *Æsop*, who, enamored with the Foxes newfangles, forsooke all hopes of life to leape into a new occupation, and these men, renowncing all possibilities of credit or estimation, to intermeddle with Italian translations.

This passage from Nash seems to indicate that these translations of Seneca proved of great use to the popular playwrights, and especially to Kyd, at whom the satire was probably aimed.[2] The *Spanish*

---

2 See F. S. Boas, *The Works of Thomas Kyd*. Introd., pp. xx—xxiv. Professor Boas states as his opinion that "though Nash grossly exaggerates Kyd's debt to 'English Seneca,' it had a strong influence upon his dramatic work." (p. xxiv.)

Tragedy contains paraphrases of passages from Seneca (*e.g.* Act iii, Sc. i, ll. 1—11, an adaptation of *Agam.* ll. 57—73), but these do not show clearly the influence of the translations, and the Latin quotations from Seneca which abound in Act iii, Sc. xiii of the same play indicate that Kyd may have gone straight to the original.

As with Kyd, so with the other Elizabethan dramatists it is almost impossible to distinguish how much of the debt which they undoubtedly owe to Seneca is due to the plays in the original, and how much to the translations. As Cunliffe observes, the more learned dramatists would not need the help of translations, while the less learned who were glad of the aid afforded by Heywood and his fellow-translators, would prefer to disguise their obligations by not quoting verbatim. Undoubtedly these translations must have done much to spread a general knowledge of Seneca, and to inspire interest in his treatment of the drama, and in all probability their influence was much greater than any examination merely of parallel passages in them and in Elizabethan plays would lead us to suspect.[1]

Though it is in this influence that their chief value lies, the plays have a certain interest of their own. Much of the verse is mere doggerel, but the style of the translators has a racy and vigorous character which often makes the reader forget its metrical imperfections. In the sixth and seventh decades of the sixteenth century Englishmen had not yet found a fitting mode of expression for the

---

[1] Cp. *Camb. Hist. of Eng. Lit.*, Vol. v, p. 80. "In any case, their influence upon writers for the popular stage is beyond doubt."

new life surging within them. Yet the life was there, however grotesquely and clumsily it might show itself, and even its early manifestations are worthy of attention.

Moreover these translations afford valuable testimony as to the grammar, metre, and vocabulary used by men of classical learning at the beginning of Elizabeth's reign. Some of the words employed are very curious and interesting, and the various grammatical forms deserve careful study.

At the same time it must be admitted that the intrinsic dramatic worth of the plays is small. The translators had before them an original which, highly as they esteemed it, was utterly lacking in true dramatic quality, and though they felt themselves at liberty to alter and adapt it on occasions, their alterations show that they had no perception of the essentials of great drama.

Seneca's plays are hardly drama at all in the true sense of the word. They show rhetoric, eloquence, and a facility for epigrams, but, in the main, have little action and less development of character. Seneca's utter inferiority to the Greek dramatists, when handling the same themes, is abundantly illustrated by the *Medea*. In certain other plays, *e.g.* in the *Hippolytus*, Seneca has altered the story in such a way as completely to ruin its tragic beauty, but in the *Medea* he has followed Euripides almost exactly in the construction of the plot, and yet has contrived to vulgarise and degrade the whole conception. In the first scene Medea appears as almost a raving maniac, calling down vengeance on her husband, and her language is as wild and extravagant at the beginning of the play as at the end. There is none

8

of the subtle development of character which we find
in Euripides, who shows us Medea as a woman
whose latent barbaric instincts gradually assert
themselves under the injuries heaped on her, till at
last the loving wife and mother becomes the furious
savage. In Euripides' play, she is by no means
wholly horrible; at first we sympathise with her
against her foes, and though at last we shudder at
her crime, we feel that the guilt is Jason's as much,
nay perhaps more, than hers. But in Seneca's play
she awakens no sympathy, for she is nothing
but a savage from beginning to end, except perhaps in one interview with Jason. In the very
first scene she announces her intention of murder-
ing her children, and thus the sense of gradually
growing horror with which Euripides leads up to
that resolve, is entirely lost. The beautiful scene
in which she suddenly bursts into tears before
Jason over her children, is wanting in Seneca,
and finally she kills the children on the stage
before their father's eyes—a gratuitous piece of
theatrical horror carefully avoided by Euripides. It
can hardly be said that the Elizabethan translators
show any greater sense of dramatic fitness than does
Seneca himself, in fact, they often accentuate his
faults and obscure his merits. Seneca's speeches,
though not well adapted to the characters in whose
mouths they are put, are generally effective from a
rhetorical point of view, containing much eloquence
and many striking epigrams. Unfortunately Studley
and his companions exaggerated Seneca's eloquence
till it became mere rant, and elaborated and
explained his epigrams till they lost all their point.
Two examples will show the translators' tendency to
exaggerate the violence of the original.

In the *Œdipus*, ll. 935, 936, 945—948, Seneca writes:

> Haec fatus aptat impiam capulo manum
> ensemque ducit. ' itane?...
> .. Iterum vivere atque iterum mori
> liceat, renasci semper ut totiens nova
> supplicia pendas—utere ingenio, miser '

The corresponding lines in Neville's revised translation are (*Tenne Tragedies*, f. 91 b, ll. 27, 28, f. 92 a, ll. 7—14):

> With that his bloudy fatall Blade, from out his sheath he drawes.
> And lowd he rores, with thundring voice. Thou beast why dost
>   thou pawse? . . . . .
> O that I might a thousand times, my wretched lyfe renewe
> O that I might revyve and dye by course in order dewe
> Ten hundred thousand times and more : than should I vengeance
>   take
> Upon this wretched head   Than I perhaps in part should make
> A meete amends in deede, for this my fowle and lothsome Sin.
> Than should the proofe of payne reprove the life that I live in.
> The choyse is in thy hand thou wretch, than use thine owne dis-
>   cretion
> And finde a meanes, whereby thou maist come to extreame con-
>   fusion.

Again, Seneca puts into Medea's mouth the words

> pelle femineos metus
> et inhospitalem Caucasum mente induc
> quodcumque vidit Pontus aut Phasis nefas,
> videbit Isthmos. effera ignota horrida,
> tremenda caelo pariter ac terris mala
> mens intus agitat.

This is rant enough surely, but Studley is determined to improve on his original. His version runs thus:

> Exile all foolysh Female feare, and pity from thy mynde,
> And as th' untamed Tygers use to rage and raue unkynde,
> That haunt the croking combrous Caves, and clumpred frosen
>   cliues,
> And craggy Rockes of Caucasus, whose bitter cold depryues
> The soyle of all Inhabitours, permit to lodge and rest,
> Such saluage brutish tyranny within thy brasen brest.

10

What euer hurly burly wrough doth Phasis understand,
What mighty monstrous bloudy feate I wrought by Sea or Land :
The like in Corynth shal be seene in most outragious guise,
Most hyddious, hatefull, horrible, to heare or see wyth eyes,
Most divelish, desperate, dreadfull deede, yet neuer knowne
before,
Whose rage shall force heauen, earth, and hell to quake and
tremble sore

(Tenne Tragedies, 120b, 9—20)

Two examples will illustrate how much some of Seneca's concise and pointed lines lose in the translation. Seneca makes Creon say to Medea 'i, querere Colchis.' Studley translates this by

Auaunt, and yell out thy complayntes at Colchis, get thee hence.

(Tenne Trag., 124a, 12)

In *Herc. Œt.* 641, 2, where the Latin has two short lines:

quos felices Cynthia vidit,
vidit miseros enata dies,

the English has six long ones:

Whom Moone at morne on top of Fortunes wheele
High swayed hath seene, at fulnesse of renowne,
The glading sunne hath seene his Scepter reele,
And him from high fall topsy turuey downe
At morne full merry, blith, in happy plight,
But whelmde in woes and brought to bale ere nyght.

(Tenne Trag , 198a, 19—24.)

It is unnecessary to linger over the dramatic weakness of the *Tenne Tragedies.* From one point of view their very faults are a merit. The imperfections of Senecan tragedy did good service by preventing unduly close imitation. Had the masterpieces of Æschylus, Sophocles, and Euripides become the models of Elizabethan playwrights, we might have lost our national drama, for the English genius is far removed from the Greek in character. As it

11

was, when the Elizabethans had learnt what they could from Seneca, they realised the dramatic weakness of his tragedies and struck out a new line for themselves. It is curious to remember that only thirty years elapsed between the publication of even the earliest of these translations and that of Marlowe's *Tamburlaine* and *Faustus*, and that within fifteen years of the appearance of the collected edition, Shakespeare had written *Romeo and Juliet*.[1] It throws a light on the extraordinarily rapid development of the English drama in those thirty or forty years. It seems a far cry from the broken-backed lines, bombastic rhetoric, and puppet figures of these Senecan translations to the perfect harmony of thought and expression, to the ageless and deathless creations of Shakespeare's plays; but great poets can never be isolated from their predecessors, and every one of the forces which had been at work in English literature had its part in the perfecting of the Elizabethan drama. Even Shakespeare might not have been quite himself as we know him, had it not been for the work of the obscure translators of Seneca.

---

[1] It should be remembered that as late as the production of *Hamlet*, Shakespeare was in touch with the Senecan tradition. There is a close parallel between the Ghost in *Hamlet* and the Ghost of Thyestes in Seneca's *Agamemnon*, who rises at the beginning of the play to incite his son Ægisthus to revenge the wrongs inflicted on him by his brother Atreus.

II.

HEYWOOD'S *TROAS, THYESTES,* AND *HERCULES FURENS.*

Jasper Heywood, the first of the translators, came of a literary family. He was the younger son of John Heywood, the epigrammatist and writer of interludes, and through his mother he was connected with Sir Thomas More[1], whilst his sister Elizabeth was the mother of John Donne. His life was more varied and adventurous than that of the other translators, and his plays show more originality and, on the whole, more poetic power, than do the other versions included in the *Tenne Tragedies.*

He was born in 1535, and sent to Oxford in 1547, at the early age of twelve. In 1554 he was elected a probationer fellow of Merton College, but in 1558 he was obliged to resign his post, and late in the same year he was elected to a fellowship at All Souls'. It was while he was a fellow of All Souls' that his Senecan translations appeared — *Troas* in 1559, *Thyestes* in 1560, and *Hercules Furens* in 1561.

It must have been immediately after the production of the last-mentioned play that Heywood was obliged to resign his fellowship at All Souls' on account of the changes in religion. The Heywood family was staunchly Catholic; Jasper's elder

---

[1] Jasper Heywood's mother, Elizabeth Rastell, was the grand-daughter of Elizabeth, sister of Sir Thomas More.

brother Ellis had already retired from Oxford to Rome, and in 1562 we find Jasper himself in the Jesuit community at Rome. After teaching philosophy and theology there for two years he was sent to the Jesuit College of Dillingen in Bavaria, where he was appointed professor of moral theology —a post which he held for seventeen years.

In 1581 he returned to England as superior of the English Jesuit Mission. In 1583 he was recalled to the Continent, but a violent gale on the voyage drove him back to the English coast, where he was arrested and carried to London in chains. A few months later he was tried with five other priests, but while they were condemned and executed, he was remanded to the Tower, and after a year [1] of strict imprisonment he was exiled to France, on pain of death if he ever again set foot in England. He spent the remaining thirteen years of his life in Burgundy, Rome, and Naples, dying at the last mentioned on January 9, $159\frac{7}{8}$.[2]

Heywood's three translations seem to have been very favourably received, and his *Troas* was the only one of the *Tenne Tragedies* which passed through two separate editions (1559 and 1563). The other translators speak of his work with evident admiration. Studley goes so far as to say that "the other Tragedies which are set furthe by Jasper Heiwood and Alexander Neuyle, are so excellently well done that in reading of them it semeth to me no translation, but euen

---

[1] The *Dict. of Nat. Biog.* states that he endured seventeen months of imprisonment in the Tower, but according to the dates given in the same article, he cannot have spent a full year in the Tower.

[2] I regret that the edition of Heywood's translations, with an introduction by H. de Vocht, which Prof. Bang has promised us in his *Materialien*, has not yet appeared, as it will doubtless throw fresh light on Heywood's adventurous career.

Seneca hymselfe to speke in englysh."[1] The praises
which T. B. in his introductory verses to Studley's
Agamemnon (see above, p. 4) bestows on Heywood's
"perfect verse" and "smouth and fyled style" seem
somewhat excessive, but it must be remembered that
Troas appeared in the first year of Elizabeth's reign,
when English versification had not yet mastered the
lessons which Wyatt and Surrey had tried to teach
it, and when Sidney and Spenser were still in their
infancy.   There is much that is grotesque in
Heywood's work, but he compares very favourably
with his fellow translators, and in one play at least
—the *Troas*—he shows real poetic feeling.   Amid all
the rant and fury of Hercules, Œdipus, Medea, and
their companions, the scene between Andromache,
her little son, and Ulysses in Act III of the *Troas* is
conspicuous for its tenderness and pathos, and
though this may be due in part to the fact that the
play itself is one of Seneca's best, credit must be
given to Heywood's judgment in selecting it for his
first attempt.   "I have," he says in his preface,
"privately taken the part which pleasĕd me best of
so excellent an author, for better is tyme spent in
the best then other.'

Heywood's style is much more free from words of
a colloquial, dialectal, or archaic character than that
of Studley, Nuce, or Newton. His English is on the
whole that of the ordinary Elizabethan translator,
though he has some striking Latinisms, such as
'freate,' 'frete' = 'sea' (Lat *fretum*), and 'roge' =
'funeral pyre' (Lat. *rogus*), which in one passage
of the 1581 edition (*T. T.* 99a, 27) has been misunder-
stood by the printer and appears as 'rage.'

It is interesting to note the change in Heywood's attitude towards his original in his successive translations. In the *Troas*, the earliest of the three, he dealt with it very freely, adding a chorus of sixty lines of his own invention at the end of Act I, a new scene consisting of a speech of ninety-one lines by the ghost of Achilles at the beginning of Act II, and three additional stanzas at the end of the chorus which concludes Act II. He also substituted a chorus of his own for the Senecan chorus at the close of Act III. In his preface 'To the Reader (*T. T.*, 95b, 96a), Heywood speaks of these alterations in the following terms :—

Now as conceımnge sondrye places augmented and some altered in this my translatıon. First forasmuch as this worke seemed unto mee in some places vnperfıte, whether left so of the Author, or parte of it loste, as tyme devoureth all thıngs, I wot not, I haue (where I thought good) with addıtıon of myne owne Penne supplıed the wante of some thynges, as the fııste Chorus, after the fyrste acte   Also in the seconde Acte I haue added the Speache of Achılles Sprıght, rysıng from Hell to requıre the Sacrıfyce of Polyxena.. .Agayne the thıee laste staues of the Chorus after the same Acte : and as foı the thyrde Chorus which in Seneca begınneth thus, Que vocat sedes? For as much as nothıng ıs therein but a heaped number of faıı e and stıaunge Countfrıes, consıderynge with my selfe, that the names of so manye vnknowen Countreyes, Mountaynes, Deseıtes, and Woodes, shoulde have no grace in the Englıshe tounge, but bee a straunge and vnpleasant thınge to the Readeıs (exceptc I should expound the Hıstoıyes of each one, which would be farıe to tedıous), I haue in the place theıeof maɗc another begınnınge in this manner. O Ioue that leadst, etc   Which alteration may be borne wıthall, seynge that Chorus is no paıt of the substaunce of the matter   In the rest I haue for my slender learnınge endeuored to keepe touch with the Latten, not worde for worde or veıse for verse, as to expounde ıt, but neglectynge the placınge of the wordes, obscrued their sence.

In the *Thyestes* Heywood has only added one original speech, the soliloquy of Thyestes at the close of the play, in which the unhappy father invokes on himself all the torments of hell.

In the *Hercules Furens*, published in 1561, there is no addition of original matter, and it is clear from the character of the translation itself that Heywood no longer "endevored to keepe touch with the Latten, not worde for worde or verse for verse, but neglectynge the placinge of the wordes, observed their sence," but that his aim was to reproduce the Latin much more closely. On the title-page he states, first in Latin, then in English, that the tragedy is "newly perused and of all faultes whereof it did before abound diligently corrected, and for the profit of young schollers so faithfully translated into English metre, that ye may se verse for verse tourned as farre as the phrase of the English permitteth."

It may be doubted whether this change in Heywood's method of translation was really beneficial to his work. In striving to keep the Latin order of words, his English becomes clumsy and frequently obscure, *e g.*, $\overline{Herc.}$ *Fur.*, D 1, *T. T.*, 5a, 9, 10:

> Nor handes that well durst enterprise his noble travayles all
> The filthy labour made to shrynke of foule Augias hall,

where 'labour' is the nominative, and 'handes' the accusative. Or *Herc. Fur.*, I 1, *T. T.*, 13a, 31—34:

> As gret as when comes houre of longer night,
> And willyng quiet sleepes to bee extent,
> Holds equal Libra Phoebus Chariots light,
> A sorte the secrete Ceres doo frequent,

where the meaning is difficult to grasp without the Latin:

> quanta, cum longae redit hora nocti
> crescere et somnos cupiens quietos
> Libra Phoebeos tenet aequa currus,
> turba secretam Cererem frequentat.

The attempt to reproduce exactly Latin con-

17

structions is not always very happy, *e.g.*, *T. T.*, 5b, 8—10, *Herc. Fur.*, D 3, 6: [1]

>   . . . . . and beaten with thy stroake
> The mount, now here, now there fell downe and rampier
>   iente of stay,
> The raging brooke of Thessaly did roon a newe found way,

where the last clause is an attempt to follow the Latin:

>   et rupto aggere
> nova cucurrit Thessalus torrens via,

and *T. T.*, 7a, 16, 17, *Herc. Fur.*, E 3:

>   .   what should I the mothers speake
> Both suffring, and aduentring gyltes?

which represents the Latin

>   . .   . quid matres loquar
> passas et ausas scelera?

and *T. T.*, 14a, 15, 16, *Herc. Fur.*, I 3:

> Hee ouer Foordes of Tartare brought
> Returnde appeased beeinge Hell,

which represents:

> Transvectus vada Tartari
> pacatis redit inferis

This close attention to the construction of the original has influenced Heywood's metre, for the attempt to represent one Latin line by one English, whilst keeping the Latin order of words, has resulted in much enjambement, and in a consequent placing of the cæsura earlier in the line than is its normal position. One passage from Megara's speech at the beginning of Act II (*T. T.*, 4b, 3—10, *Herc. Fur.*, c 6) will illustrate this:

---

[1] A mistake has been made in the binding of the 1561 edition. D 6 occupies the place of D 4.

. . . To mee yet neuer day
Hath careles shin'de the ende of one affliction past away
Beginning of an other is: an other ennemy
Is forthwith founde, before that hee his joyfull family
Retourne vnto an other fyght hee taketh by behest
Nor any respite giuen is to him nor quiet rest
But whyle that he commaunded is straight him pursueth shee
The hatefull Iuno

The extent of the alteration produced in
Heywood's rhythm may be gauged by the different
proportion of lines with the main pause after the
second or third foot to be found in the *Hercules
Furens* as compared with the *Troas*. Metrically,
the ear requires the cæsura after the fourth foot,
and there is usually a slight pause at that place,
but the main pause (or, as it may be called, the
logical cæsura as distinct from the metrical) often
occurs earlier in the line, and in the *Troas* the
proportion of lines in which it is to be found after
the second foot is under six per cent. of the total
number of fourteeners, whilst in the *Hercules Furens*
it is over twenty-two per cent. Again, in the *Troas*
the number of lines with the logical cæsura after
the third foot is under two per cent., whilst in the
Hercules Furens it is over six per cent. Thus in
the latter play, the number of normal lines in which
the logical and metrical cæsuras coincide in falling
after the fourth foot, has enormously decreased.

III.

NEVILLE'S *ŒDIPUS.*

Alexander Neville, the translator of the *Œdipus,* was born in 1544. He was the son of Richard Neville, of South Leverton, Nottinghamshire, and his mother was the daughter of Sir Walter Mantell and sister of Margaret, the mother of Barnabe Googe. Alexander's younger brother, Thomas Neville, had a distinguished career, becoming Dean, first of Peterborough, then of Canterbury, and Master of Trinity College, Cambridge.

Alexander seems to have entered at Cambridge at the early age of twelve, for we find that he graduated B.A. in 15$\frac{6}{3}$. It was in 1560 that he translated the *Œdipus* according to his prefatory letter to Wotton, though it did not appear in print till 1563.[1] After leaving Cambridge he studied law in London, where he made the acquaintance of George Gascoigne. He was one of the "five sundry Gentlemen" who required Gascoigne "to write in verse somewhat worthye to bee remembred, before he entered into their fellowshippe," and he proposed the Latin motto, *Sat cito,*

---

[1] In 1563 Neville also contributed commendatory verses to the *Eglogs* of Barnabe Googe, who was his cousin, not his uncle, as the *Dict. of Nat. Biog.* erroneously states.

si sat bene, on which Gascoigne composed "seven Sonets in seq[u]ence."

Neville became secretary to Archbishop Parker, and remained in the service of Parker's successors, Grindal and Whitgift. In 1575 he published a Latin account of Kett's rebellion of 1549, to which he appended a description of Norwich and its antiquities, and in 1587 there appeared *Academiæ Cantabrigiensis lacrymæ tumulo . . . P. Sidney sacratæ per A. Nevillum*. The *Dict of Nat Biog*. suggests that he may be identified with the Alexander Neville who sat in Parliament as M.P. for Christchurch, Hampshire, in 1585, and for Saltash in 1601. He died in 1614, and was buried in Canterbury Cathedral, where Thomas Neville, then Dean of Canterbury, erected a monument to commemorate his brother and himself.

The title page of the first edition of Neville's *Œdipus* runs thus.—

"The Lamentable Tragedie of Œdipus the Sonne of Laius Kyng of Thebes out of Seneca. By Alexander Neuyle. Imprynted at London in seint Brydes Churchyarde: ouer-agaynst the North doore of the Churche: by Thomas Colwell. 1563. 28 Aprilis."

Then follows a dedicatory epistle "To the ryght Honorable Maister Doctor Wotton: One of the Quenes Maiesties priuye Counsayle," which occupies four pages. This is followed by "The Preface to the Reader," occupying seven pages, after which comes the list of *dramatis personæ*. The translation occupies eighty-three pages, and is followed by a page containing a list of errata, and the colophon.

---

1 See Gascoigne. *Posies   Flowers.   Gascoigne's Memories*

The volume[1] is a small octavo with the collation a⁸ A—E⁸ F².

Neville's translation of the *Œdipus* possesses particular interest for us, since it is the only one of the *Tenne Tragedies* of 1581 which had undergone a thorough revision since its first appearance. A careful comparison of the text of the first editions of Heywood, Studley, and Nuce's versions with that of these plays as they appeared in the *Tenne Tragedies* shows that the 1581 edition was merely a reprint of the earlier text With Neville's *Œdipus* the case is otherwise. It is true that no hint is given of the changes which have been made, and the title, which would lead the reader to imagine that he had here a faithful reproduction of Neville's early work, runs thus:—"Œdipus. The Fifth Tragedy of Seneca, Englished. The yeare of our Lord M.D.L.X. By Alexander Nevyle," and is followed by the dedication to Wotton and the "Preface to the Reader," which had appeared in the edition of 1563. Yet there are changes even in the dedicatory epistle to Wotton. It now opens with a reference, absent in the earlier edition, to "this sixteenth yeare of myne age" [*i.e.* 1560].

The translation itself has been practically re-written. Those critics who have consulted only the edition of 1581 have often praised the excellence of this translation of *Œdipus* when considered as the work of a youth of sixteen. Thus Warton says, "Notwithstanding the translator's youth, it is by far the most spirited and elegant version in the whole collection, and it is to be regretted that he did not

---

[1] The copy here described is that in the British Museum.
C . 34 . a . 9 (1).

undertake all the rest," and this verdict was republished in the introduction to the Spenser Society's reprint of the *Tenne Tragedies* in 1887. It is echoed by E. Jockers in his *Die englischen Seneca-Uebersetzer des 16. Jahrhunderts*—"Nevyle ist ohne Zweifel der begabteste von samtlichen Uebersetzern. Seine Uebersetzung zeigt dichterischen Schwung und jugendliche Lebendigkeit,"[1] and in a foot-note Jockers quotes Warton's judgment, and opposes Collier's less favourable estimate of Neville. Neither Jockers nor the writer of the article on Neville in the *Dictionary of National Biography* shows any knowledge of the difference between the two editions of the *Œdipus*.

Almost every line of the translation contains some alteration from the earlier version. In the edition of 1563 Neville's versification had been extremely irregular; intermingled with the regular fourteeners which formed the staple metre of his translation were lines containing twelve or sixteen syllables, unrhyming fourteeners, or even short unrhyming lines of four or six syllables. In the later edition the versification runs much more smoothly, and the greater number of the irregularities have been removed, though one or two examples remain.[2]

Changes other than metrical are also abundant. Speeches are altered and assigned to different characters,[3] lines are inserted or omitted,[4] and

---

[1] *Die englischen Seneca-Uebersetzer* p 43

[2] *e g* *Tenne Trag* 79 b, 7, 82 b, 14, 92 b, 10

[3] *e g* Iocasta's speech in Act I, 1. 22 is given to Œdipus, and 'you' is accordingly changed to 'I,' and 'that' to 'this'

[4] Act I, 1. 4 is an insertion

C

there are a large number of purely verbal alterations.[1]

The extent of the alterations may be gauged by a
comparison of some passages from Act I—

1563 EDITION.	1581 EDITION.
ll. 1—5.	ll 1—6
The night is gon & dredfull day begins at length to appeare	The Night is gon . and diedfull day begins at length t'ap-peere
And Lucifer beset wt Clowds, hymself aloft doth reare.	And Phœbus all bedim'de with Clowdes, himselfe aloft doth reere.
And gliding forth with heavy hewe. A doleful blase doth beare (in Skyes).	And glyding forth with deadly hue, a dolefull blase in Skies
Now shal the houses voide be sene, with Plagues de-uoured quight	Doth beare : Great terror & dismay to the beholders Eyes.
And slaughter yt the night hath made, shall daye brynge forth to lyght.	Now shall the houses voyde bee seene, with Plague deuoured quight ?
	And slaughter that the night hath made, shall day bring forth to light.

ll. 10—13.	ll. 11—14.
For as the mountaynes houge and hie, the blustryng windes withstand,	For as the Mountaynes huge and hie, the blustring windes withstand.
And craggy Rocks, the belch-ing fluds do dash and beate fro land.	And craggy Rocks, the belching fluds do dash, and driue fro land :
Though that the seas in quiet are and nought at all do fome :	Though that the Seas in quiet are, and calme on euery side .
So kingdoms great submytted lye, to Fortunes doulfull Dome.	So kingdoms great all Windes and Waues of Fortune must abide.

---

[1] *e g.* 'remayne' in Act I, l. 62 for 'abyde,' 'woe' in l 94 for 'grief.'

1563 EDITION	1581 EDITION
ll 28—34	ll 29—41.

This feare and only this my [read, me] dryues from fathers kingdoms great

Not lyke a wanderyng Vacabounde the wayes unknowen I beate,

But all mystrustfull of my selfe thy lawes (O Nature) for to keape

I sought the meanes Yet feare I stil and fear into my mynde doth creape

Though cause of Dread not one I se yet feare and dread I all.

And scante in credit with myself, I seke my fatal fall

(By Dome of doulful Destinies.)

For what shuld I suppose the cause ? A Plage that is so generall   .   .   .

This feare, and onely this me causde my fathers kingdome great

For to forsake.   I fled not thence when fear the minde doth beat

The restlesse thought still dreds the thing, it knows can neuer chaunce.

Such fansies now torment my heart, my safety to aduaunce,

And eke thyne euer sacred lawes (O Nature) for to keepe

A stately Scepter I forsooke, yet secret feare doth creepe

Within my breast and frets it still with doubt and discontent,

And inward pangues which secretly my thoughts a sunder rent.

So though no cause of dred I see, yet feare and dred I all,

And scant in credit with my selfe, my thoughts my mind appall

That I cannot perswaded be, though reason tell me no,

But that the Web is weauing still of my decreed wo

For what should I suppose the cause ? a Plague that is so generall   .   .

The reason for these changes is evident. In the eighteen years which had elapsed since the first publication of Neville's translation, English poetry had made marvellous progress. The standard of versification had been raised, and the halting metre which had been tolerated[1] in 1563 would in 1581 no longer pass muster, even as the work of a youth of sixteen. It may be urged that the same reason ought to have produced revised versions of the work of Heywood and Studley, but the difference between their case and that of Neville must be borne in mind. When the *Tenne Tragedies* appeared, Heywood was a Jesuit priest, exiled from England, and Studley, who was no longer a Fellow of Trinity, may also have been absent from England. In both cases the translators had been forced to give up their university careers, and had devoted themselves to the promulgation of their religious opinions, widely different as these were from each other. Neither would have desired to spend time over the revision of what he would have deemed a trifling production of his less serious youth, even if, as seems unlikely, the editor of the 1581 volume consulted them in the matter. Neville, on the other hand, had remained a scholar and was now Secretary to the Archbishop of Canterbury. He was the author of various Latin works, and his brother was one of the most distinguished Cambridge dignitaries. A drastic revision of the early translation was necessary, but even when this was complete Neville seems to have felt that the result was not altogether creditable to his mature scholarship, and he therefore sheltered himself

---

[1] T. B. in his commendatory verses prefixed to Studley's *Agamemnon* (1566) says when enumerating the translators who can rival Jasper Heywood ·

"A Neuyle also one there is, in verse that gyues no place
To Heiwood (though he be full good) in vsying of his grace."

behind the title and dedication which ascribed the work to his sixteenth year.[1]

In both its original and its revised form the translation is decidedly free. In his dedicatory epistle to Dr. Wotton, Neville excuses this freedom on the plea that he had made the translation only for the use of a few friends, who apparently wished to act it.

> For I to none other ende remoued him [*i.e.* Seneca] from his naturall and lofty style, to our corrupt and base, or as some men (but vntruly) [1563 al men] affyrme it, most barbarous Language: but onely to satisfy the instant requests of a few my familiar frends, who thought to haue put it to the very same use, that Seneca himselfe in his Inuention pretended: Which was by the tragicall and Pompous showe vpon Stage, to admonish all men of their fickle Estates, to declare the vnconstant head of wauering Fortune, her sodayne interchaunged and soone altered Face: and lyuely to expresse the iust reuenge, and fearefull punishmets of horrible Crimes, wherewith the wretched worlde in these our myserable dayes pyteously swarmeth. This caused me not to be precise [1563 to precise] in following the Author, word for word: but sometymes by addition, somtimes by subtraction, to vse the aptest Phrases in geuing the Sense that I could inuent. Whereat a great numbre (I know) will be more offended than Reason or Wysedome woulde they should bee.

It is in the choric portions that Neville has treated his original most freely. He has expanded the chorus in the first act from ninety-two lines to a hundred and seventeen, whilst he has entirely omitted the chorus of a hundred and six lines in praise of Bacchus at the close of Act II. He has replaced the chorus of fifty-five lines in Act III by a new chorus of twenty-two lines dealing with a different subject; and similarly in Act IV he has substituted a short original chorus of fourteen lines

---

[1] The edition of 1581 insists strongly on the fact, scarcely mentioned in that of 1563, that the translation was made in 1560. In the list of plays and translators at the beginning of the *Tenne Tragedies*, the only play of which the date is mentioned is Neville's *Œdipus*, to which '1560' is added.

for the Senecan one of thirty lines. The chorus in Act v is substantially the same as Seneca's, though Neville, who has a liking for moral maxims, adds four lines quite in the Senecan manner:

And thou that subiect art to death. Regard thy latter day
Thinke no man blest before his ende   Aduise thee well and stay
Be sure his lyfe, and death, and all, be quight exempt from mysery.
Ere thou do once presume to say . this man is blest and happy

(Tenne Tragedies. 92 b, 30-33.)

In the dramatic portions Neville follows his original much more closely, but he has a tendency to expand it by adding unnecessary reflections. Thus he enlarges the last speech of Œdipus from twenty lines to fifty-two by making such additions as the following:

O Œdipus accursed wretch, lament thine own Calamity,
Lament thy state, thy griefe lament, thou Caitife borne to misery.
Where wilt thou now become (alas ?) thy Face where wilt thou
    hyde .
O myserable Slaue, canst thou such shamefull tormentes byde?

(Tenne Tragedies. 94 a, 7-10)

After the messenger's description, a little earlier in the same act, of the despair of Œdipus and his plucking out of his own eyes, Neville puts these moral lines into the messenger's mouth:

Beware betimes, by him beware, I speake vnto you all.
Learne Iustice, truth, and feare of God by his vnhappy fall.

(Tenne Tragedies 92 b, 11, 12)

A full account of Neville's divergences from the Latin in the revised edition of 1581 will be found in Jockers *Die englischen Seneca-Uebersetzer*, pp. 44—62.

It will be seen from the extracts already given that Neville has all the Elizabethan readiness to point a moral, accentuated by his extreme youth when he first undertook the translation of the

Œdipus. The 'Preface to the Reader' which appeared in the edition of 1563, and was reprinted verbatim in that of 1581, shows that he approached his task with the moral severity and censoriousness of sixteen years' experience of life. Moral in their aims as are the other translators of Seneca, they cannot equal Neville, who sees in the unfortunate Œdipus only " a dredfull Example of Gods horrible vengeance for sinne", and a suitable warning for "our present Age, wherein Vice hath chiefest place, & Vertue put to flight, lies as an abiect, languishing in great extremity."

IV.

STUDLEY'S *AGAMEMNON, MEDEA, HER-CULES ŒTÆUS*, AND *HIPPOLYTUS*.

John Studley's career presents in some respects a curious parallel to that of Jasper Heywood. Both translators were University men, fellows of colleges, whose versions of Seneca were their first essays in literature. Though their religious opinions were widely different—Heywood being a Roman Catholic and Studley a Puritan—they both lost their fellowships on account of those opinions, and in after life both abandoned classical scholarship for theological controversy.

John Studley was one of the original scholars of Westminster School,[1] and the first to be elected to Cambridge. In the Cambridge University Register it is stated that he matriculated as a pensioner at Trinity College, 12 May, 1563, and proceeded B.A. 156$\frac{6}{7}$, and M.A. 1570. According to the books of Trinity College, he became a minor fellow, 8 Sept., 1567, and a major fellow, 7 April, 1570.

At this time the Master of Trinity was the famous Dr. Whitgift, afterwards Archbishop of Canterbury, a High Churchman and strict disciplinarian, who was chiefly responsible for certain new statutes of the University which were aimed

---

[1] *Alumni Westmonast*, p 45. See also Studley's *Agamemnon* (1566), dedicatory epistle to Sir W. Cecil.

against the Puritans. Trinity College also contained the leader of the Puritan faction, Thomas Cartwright, Lady Margaret Professor of Divinity, and party feeling must have been extremely bitter within the college.

Strype's *Life of Whitgift*, which gives us a lively picture of the internal dissensions of the University at this time, tells us that there was "a great faction in Trinity College of such as were disaffected to the present ecclesiastical settlement, which created the Master no small trouble and disquiet" It appears that in 1572 Whitgift thought of resigning his post on account of these dissensions. In Strype's words, "as he [Whitgift] was an impartial executor of the statutes of the college; so he had hereby raised the stomachs of some of the Fellows against him, who contended unkindly with him; they had treated him with so much slander, and such reviling terms, as wholly discouraged him to tarry any longer among them."[1]

It is clear that Studley belonged to this section among the Fellows. His name appears in a list of one hundred and sixty-four signatures appended to a declaration issued in 1562 in connection with the disturbances directed against the new statutes.[2] On 1 February, 157$\frac{2}{3}$, Studley and Booth, another fellow of Trinity, became sureties in the sum of £40, for John Browning,[3] also a fellow of the same

---

[1] Strype, *Life of Whitgift*, p. 51.

[2] Heywood and Wright, *Cambridge University Transactions*, Vol I, p 61

[3] Baker MS., iii, p 392 (*Harl* 7030) "Febr 1 Johes Brownyng M A Socius Col. Trin —et Hugo Boothe et Jo Studley Mri A et socii ejusdem Coll venerunt coram Tho Bynge vicecan et recognoverunt se debere Dnae Reginae viz Jo Br centum marcae —et praed: Hugo et Jo. 40lib solvend —sub conditione sequenti . ." (Then follow the conditions which Browning was to observe)

college, who had been committed to the Tolbooth for "uttering in St. Mary's certain doctrines tending to the heresy of Novatus," and for disobeying the consequent command of Whitgift and the heads of houses to abstain from preaching "till his further purgation."

By 1573 Whitgift had been persuaded to remain at Trinity, and was determined to exercise strict discipline over the refractory Fellows. Those who would not submit were obliged to leave their posts It appears from the college books that Studley ceased to be a Fellow at the end of 1573, for according to the Bursar's book for the year Michaelmas 1573-1574, he received his stipendium only for the quarter from Michaelmas to Christmas, 1573. No reason is there given for his withdrawal, but among the "extraordinary expenses" for the same year there is an item "to Mr. Studley at his departure v^{lb}," which seems to indicate that some compensation was made him for the determination of his Fellowship.[1]

Little is known of Studley's after life.[2] In 1574 he produced a translation of Bale's "Acta Pontificum Romanorum," under the title of "The Pageant of Popes, Contayninge the lyues of all the Bishops of

---

[1] For this information I am indebted to the kindness of Mr. Aldis Wright, Vice-Master of Trinity College, Cambridge.

[2] Richard Robinson, in his *Rewarde of Wickednesse* (1574), mentions Studley in such a way as to imply that the latter belonged to the Inns of Court. After seeing Helen of Troy, Medea, Pope Alexander the Sixth, and others in hell, and "Skelton and Lydgat, Wagei, Heywood, and Barnabe Googe" in the garden of the Muses on Helicon, Robinson is commanded by the Muses to write what Morpheus has shown him in a book. He excuses himself by saying

Your Honours haue in Th'innes of Court, a sort of Gentlemen,
That fine would fit your whole intentes, with stately stile to Pen
Let Studley, Hake, or Fulwood take, that William hath to name,
This piece of worke in hande, that bee more fitter for the same.

Rome, from the beginninge of them to the yeare of
Grace 1555 . . . . Shewing manye straunge,
notorious, outragious, and tragicall partes played by
them the like whereof hath not els bin hearde. both
pleasant and profitable for this age. Written in
Latin by Maister Bale, and now Englished with
sondrye additions by I. S "

Chetwood states that Studley was "killed in
Flanders at the Siege of Breda having a command
under Prince Maurice, in 1587."[1]   Not much reliance
can be placed on this statement.   The siege of Breda
took place in 1590, and it is clear that Chetwood's
information with regard to Studley was not very
accurate, for the latter is described as having been
educated at Oxford, and only two of his translations
are mentioned.

Studley's translations of Seneca's *Agamemnon*
and *Medea* both appeared in 1566, though it is clear
that *Agamemnon* must have preceded *Medea* by
some months.   The introductory verses and dedication prefixed to *Agamemnon* show that this was, as
Studley terms it, "The fyrst frutes" of his "good
will and trauaile."   Thomas Nuce, Thomas Delapeend,
W. R, H. C, and the other writers who contribute
prefatory verses to the translation, all implore the
reader's indulgence on account of Studley's youth
and inexperience.   Apparently *Agamemnon* was
favourably received, for the introductory matter
prefixed to *Medea* is much shorter, and in his
"Preface to the Reader" Studley says "If I had not
gentle Reader a better truste in thy gentlenesse,
then affyaunce in myne own weakenesse, I had

---

[1] *The British Theatre Containing the Lives of the English
Dramatic Poets* (1750), p 7.

not assayed thys second attempte, to bewraye my rudenesse and ignoraunce unto thy skilfull iudgemente." Both *Agamemnon* and *Medea* were entered to Thomas Colwell the printer in the Stationers' Register for the year July 1565—July 1566, but the mention of *Medea* occurs seventy entries after that of *Agamemnon*.

The title of *Agamemnon* runs thus :—

The Eyght Tragedie of Seneca. Entituled Agamemnon Translated out of Latin in to English, by Iohn Studley, Student in Trinitie Colledge in Cambridge. Imprinted at London in Fletestreat, beneath the Conduit, at the signe of S Iohn Euangelyst, by Thomas Colwell Anno Domini, M. D LXVI.

The volume is a small octavo with the collation ¶⁸, A⁴, B—G⁸. The first twenty-four pages are occupied by commendatory verses in Latin and English, by Thomas Newce (or Nuce), W. R., H. C., Thomas Delapeend, W. Parkar, and T. B. These are followed by a dedication to Sir William Cecil, and a preface to the reader. The text occupies ninety-six pages, and is followed by a list of errata.

In the edition of 1581 *Agamemnon* occupies the eighth place among the translations. All the introductory matter is omitted, and a short Argument in prose takes its place. The text is evidently reprinted from that of the 1566 edition. A few misprints have been corrected, but others have been introduced, and there is no change of any importance.

Medea appeared as a small octavo volume, similar in size to *Agamemnon*. The title-page runs thus :—

The seuenth Tragedie of Seneca, Entituled Medea: Translated out of Latin into English, by Iohn Studley, Student in Trinitie Colledge in Cambridge. Imprinted at London in Fleetestreate, beneth the Conduit, at the Signe of Sainct Iohn Euangelist, by Thomas Colwell. Anno Domini M. D. LXVI.

The volume has the collation [A⁴] B—G⁸. The first eight pages are occupied by the title, the dedication to the Earl of Bedford, the preface to the reader, a poem by W. F. "in the Translatours behalfe," the argument (in verse), and the list of *dramatis personæ*. The text occupies ninety-five pages, and the last page is occupied by a wood-cut.

In the *Tenne Tragedies* of 1581 *Medea* has the seventh place. The text is the same as that of the 1566 edition, save for unimportant variants in spelling and punctuation, with the solitary exception of Act II, l. 43, which has "it redresse" for "remedye it" of the earlier edition.

Studley also translated Seneca's *Hippolytus* and *Hercules Œtæus*, and his versions of these plays occupy the fourth and tenth places respectively in the *Tenne Tragedies* of 1581. No separate edition of either translation is extant, but it seems probable that such existed, as in the case of *Agamemnon* and *Medea*; and there are entries in the Stationers' Register which lend colour to such a supposition. The second entry for the year July 1566—July 1567 runs thus—

"Recevyd of henry Denham for his lycence for the pryntinge of a boke intituled the IXᵗʰ and Xᵗʰ tragide of Lucious Anneus [Seneca] oute of the laten into englisshe by T W fellowe of Pembrek Hall in Chambryge"

We know that "the IXᵗʰ tragide," i e. *Octavia*, was translated by T. N., and was published by Henry Denham in quarto. Copies of this quarto exist in the British Museum and the Bodleian Library, but they are undated. This version was reprinted in the 1581 collected edition of the *Tenne Tragedies*, where it was ascribed to Thomas Nuce, at one time Fellow of

Pembroke Hall, Cambridge. No other Elizabethan translation of the *Octavia* is extant.

It seems probable that T. W. in the Stationers' Register is a mistake for T. N., and that this entry refers to a contemplated issue of *Octavia*, and of *Hercules Œtæus*—the latter being generally known as the tenth tragedy of Seneca. The title of *Herc. Œt.* in the 1581 edition states that it was "translated out of Latin into Englishe by I. S."; and the list at the beginning of the volume ascribes it, together with *Hippolytus, Medea,* and *Agamemnon,* to John Studley. We know from Nuce's commendatory verses prefixed to Studley's *Agam.* that the two men were on friendly terms, and the translations may both have been entered as his by mistake. In 1570 "the iij parte of Hercules Oote" was entered in the Stationers' Register to Thomas Colwell, who had printed *Agam.* and *Medea* for Studley. Does this imply that Colwell had in some way interfered with the printing of *Herc. Œt.* by Denham, and is the mention of the "third part" an indication that this was the third of Seneca's tragedies which Colwell published? [1]

No separate edition of *Hippolytus* is extant. There is an entry in the Stationers' Register, July 1566-7, considerably later in the year than the entry of the "IXth and Xth Tragedie," which runs: "Recevyd of henry Denham for his lycense for ye pyrntinge of the iiijth parte Seneca Workes." *Hippolytus* is described in the 1581 quarto as "The fourth and most ruthful tragedy of L. Annæus Seneca," and it seems probable that this entry refers to an early edition of the translation, especially as for Aug. 31, 1579 we find

---

[1] For this suggestion I am indebted to Dr. W. W Greg.

the following entry: "Ric. Jones. John Charlwood. Allowed unto them by the consent of henry Denham these copies folowing which they bought of him. The Arbor of Amytye. Turberville's songes and sonnettes. The fourthe Tragedie of Seneca."

If these surmises are correct as to the identity of *Herc. Œt.* and *Hipp* with the works entered in the Stationers' Register, Studley's four translations must have been published within a short time of each other. This inference is strengthened by their similarities in style and diction, whilst it is interesting to observe the development in Studley's use of the fourteener. In the later plays there is an increasing number of lines in which the fourth foot ends in the middle of a word, so that it is impossible for the cæsura to retain its normal place, *e.g.*

> Bryng in your scratting pawes a bui-[1]
> nyng biande of deadly fyre.
>
> (*Medea* (1566), B 1ᵛ)

Agamemnon has 7 such lines out of a total of 1148 fourteeners, *Medea* 10 out of 1257, *Hercules Œtæus* 36 out of 1688, and *Hippolytus* 37 out of 1271.

Studley's poetical style differs widely from that of Heywood. The diction of his four translations is extremely interesting; there is a homely and popular character about it which is quite foreign to Heywood's, though we find it again in some measure in Newton's *Thebais*. His dramatic powers and sense of poetic fitness do not seem to have been of a high order. He often falls into bathos exactly in the

---

[1] So printed in the 1566 edition, which always divides the four-teener into two lines of print, generally at the end of the fourth foot. When that foot ends in the middle of a word, in some cases as here the word is divided, in others the division takes place after the word.

passages where he wishes to be impressive; in fact, his translations offer more examples of bathos than any of the others included in the *Tenne Tragedies*.

It is difficult to make a selection where the choice is so wide, but the following lines may be quoted from Cassandra's vision of the murder of Agamemnon (*T. T.*, 156a, 15—26. *Ag.*, F 7ᵛ):

The King in gorgyous royall robes on chayre of State doth sit,
And pranckt with pryde of Pryams pomp of whom he conqueid it.
Put of this hostile weede, to him (the Queene, his Wyfe gan say,)
And of thy louing Lady wrought weare rather thys aray.
This garment knit. It makes mee loth, that shiuering heere I
stande
O shall a King be murthered, by a banisht wretches hande?
Out, shall Th'adulterer destroy the husbande of the Wyfe?
The dreadfull destinies approcht, the foode that last in lyfe
He tasted of before his death, theyr maysters bloud shall see,
The gubs of bloude downe diopping on the wynde shall powred
bee
By traytious tricke of trapping weede his death is broughs
about,
Which being put upon his heade his handes coulde not get out

After an interview with Jason, Medea is made to say:

What is he slily slypt and gon? falles out the matter so?
O Iason dost thou sneake away, not hauing minde of mee,
Nor of those former great good turnes that I haue done for thee?
T. T., 131a, 24—26. *Medea*, E 3ᵛ

Hercules when recalling his former prowess exclaims:

I that returnde from dennes of death, and Stigian streame defyed
And ferryed ouer Lethes lake, and diagd up, chaind, and tyde
The tryple headded mastiffe hownd, when Tytans teeme did start
So at the ougly sight that he fel almost from his cart.
Herc Œt, *T T.*, 206a, 7—10.

It seems unkind to dwell on Studley's poetical failings. He is certainly no great poet, but occasionally he has some fine lines. In the last scene of the *Hippolytus* the Chorus says (*Hipp.*, *T. T.*, 74 b, 27):

O Theseus to thy plaint eternall tyme is graunted thee,

and there is pathos in Theseus' cry over the dead body of his son :

> Lo I enioy my fathers gift, O solitarinesse.

Such lines however are rare, and the chief attractions of Studley's verse seem to be its quaintness and its exuberance. Both these qualities have been exemplified in the quotations already given, but one quotation more may be adduced, from the description of Medea practising her magic arts :

> She mumbling coniures up by names of ills the rable rout,
> In hugger mugger cowched long, kept close, vnserched out :
> All pestlent plagues she calles upon, what euer Libie lande,
> In frothy boyling stream doth worke, or muddy belching sande
> What tearing torrents Taurus breedes, with snowes unthawed stil
> Where winter flawes, and hory frost knit hard the craggy hill,
> She layes her crossing hands upon each monstrous coniurde thing,
> And ouer it her magicke verse with charming doth she sing :
> A mowsie, rowsie, rusty route with cancred Scales Iclad
> From musty, fusty, dusty dens where lurked long they had
> Doe craull. . . .
>
> T. T., 133 a, 9—19, Medea, E 7ᵛ , 8.

With regard to Studley's treatment of his original, it may be noted that in no play has he made such extensive alterations as were effected by Heywood in the *Troas*, whilst on the other hand he nowhere follows the Latin as closely as Heywood does in the *Hercules Furens.* His chief additions of original matter are in *Medea* (*T. T.*, 121 a, 1—122 a, 9), where he substitutes a Chorus of his own for the Senecan Chorus; in *Agamemnon* (*T. T.*, 159 b, 17—160 b, 20), where he adds a speech by Eurybates in which the death of Cassandra, the flight of Orestes, and the imprisonment of Electra are narrated; and in *Hippolytus* (*T. T.*, 73 b, 15—34), where he introduces a curious passage in which Phædra implores the spirit of Hippolytus to take her living body in exchange for his own mutilated corpse.

D

In general, Studley follows the meaning of the Latin fairly closely, but does not try to reproduce the Latin order as Heywood does, and he frequently expands, and explains wherever he considers it necessary, *e.g.*, where Seneca makes Medea say of Jason:

> merita contempsit mea
> qui scelere flammas viderat vinci et mare?

Studley has (*T. T.*, 122a, 16—23, *Medea*, B 5ᵛ, 6):

> O hath he such a stony heart, that doth no more esteeme,
> The great good turnes, and benefits that I imployde on him?
> Who knowes that I have lewdly used enchauntments for his sake,
> The rigour rough, and stormy rage, of swelling Seas to slake.
> The grunting firy foming Bulles, whose smoking guts were stuft,
> With smoltring fumes, that from theyr Iawes, and nosthrils out they puft.
> I stopt their gnashing mounching mouths, I quencht their burning breath,
> And vapors hot of stewing paunch, that els had wrought his death.

In one or two cases it seems evident that Studley has mistranslated the Latin through haste or carelessness, *e.g.*, in *T. T.*, 149a, 3, 4, *Ag.*, D 4, he translates Seneca's—

> tu pande vivat coniugis frater mei
> et pande teneat quas soror sedes mea

by—

> Declare if that my brothers wyfe enioy the vytall ayre
> And tel me to what kind of Coast my sister doth repayre.

In *Herc. Œt.*, *T. T.*, 202a, 13—

> Nocens videri qui petit mortem cupit

is represented by—

> He doth condemne himselfe to dye that needes will guylty seeme.

V.

NUCE S *OCTAVIA*.

Thomas Nuce, or Newce, as his name is sometimes spelt, was educated at Pembroke Hall, Cambridge. He graduated B A. in 1561, M.A. in 1565, B D in 1572 [1] The *Dict. of Nat. Biog.* states that in 1562 he was a Fellow of Pembroke, and that some time after 1563 he became rector of Cley, Norfolk. In course of time he was appointed to several other livings, all of them in Norfolk and Suffolk, and from February 158⅘ till his death he was a Prebend of Ely Cathedral. He died in 1617, and was buried in Gazeley Church.

Nuce contributed fourteen Latin hexameters and a hundred and seventy-two lines of English verse in praise of Studley's version of the *Agamemnon* (1566) He himself published a translation of the *Octavia*, of which the title runs thus:

The ninth Tragedie of Lucius Annens Seneca, called Octavia, Translated out of Latine into English, by T N Student in Cambridge Imprinted at London, by Henry Denham

The volume is a small quarto, with the collation A⁴ (A 1 wanting), B—G⁴, one leaf unsigned (? A 1). The translation is preceded by a dedicatory epistle "To the Right Honorable, the Lorde Robert Dudley, Earle of Leicester," which begins "After that I had waded, right honorable, in the translating of this Tragedy called *Octavia*, written first in Latine by that notable and sententious Poet *Seneca*," and describes the translation as a "smal combrous trifle" and as the "rude and

---

[1] For this information I am indebted to J. N Keynes, D Sc , Registrary of the University of Cambridge

vnsauorie first fruits of my yong study" This is
followed by a short and modest preface "To the
Reader," and by a rhymed "argument" of the play,
and a list of *dramatis personæ*. The translation
occupies 49 pages, and is followed by a list of errata.
The colophon, like the title-page, gives no indication
as to date.[1]

The only evidence which we possess with regard
to the date of this edition is an entry in the
Stationers' Register for the year July 1566—July
1567, which has already been mentioned in the
chapter on Studley's translations. It runs thus:

Recevyd of henry Denham for his lycence for the pryntinge of
a boke intituled the IXth and Xth tragide of Lucious Anneus [Seneca]
oute of the laten into englisshe by T W fellowe of Pembrek Hall
in Chambryge

The *Octavia* was always known as the ninth
tragedy of Seneca, and T W is probably a misprint
for T. N., the initials which stand on the title-page
of the *Octavia*, and which are explained in the 1581
edition as representing T. Nuce. An explanation of
the " Xth tragide " mentioned in the entry has
already been suggested. Hence this translation may
be assigned with some probability to 1566-7. I have
been unable to find any foundation for the con-
jectural date 1561 assigned to it in the article on
Nuce in the *Dict. of Nat. Biog.*; and as in the same
article the date of Studley's *Agamemnon* (1566) is
wrongly given as 1561, it seems probable that in
Nuce's case also 1561 is merely a slip for 1566, the
year assigned to the *Octavia* by Warton, who is one
of the authorities mentioned at the close of the
article.

---

[1] The copy here described is that in the British Museum,
C. 34, c. 48

The *Octavia* occupied the ninth place in the collected edition of 1581. The text is the same as that of the earlier edition. The Argument is retained, but the dedicatory epistle and the preface to the reader are omitted. It is a curious fact that the black-letter type used in the *Octavia* is larger and clearer than that of the other plays in the volume.

The *Octavia* is an interesting play, both for its metre and language. Unlike the rest of the *Tenne Tragedies*, it does not employ the fourteener at all. Nuce apparently perceived that the fourteener was by no means an ideal metre for tragedy, and he had the courage to discard it, and to use in its place the five-foot or decasyllabic line rhyming in couplets, occasionally in triplets, and the octosyllable rhyming alternately. In Nuce's hands, as in those of other Elizabethans, the decasyllabic couplet produces a totally different effect from the 'heroic couplet' of Dryden and Pope, though it is identically the same in structure, except that it has no regular pause at the close of the couplet. A passage from *T. T.*, 162b, 5—17, *Oct.*, B 1ᵛ, 2 will illustrate Nuce's use of this metre:

> Lo see of late the great and mighty stocke,
> By lurking Fortunes sodayne forced knocke,
> Of Claudius quite subuert and cleane extinct:
> Tofore, who held the world in his precinct;
> The Brittayne Ocean coast that long was free,
> He ruld at wil, and made it to agree,
> Their Romaine Gallies great for to embrace.
> Lo, he that Tanais people first did chase,
> And Seas unknowen to any Romayne wight
> With lusty sheering shippes did overdight,
> And safe amid the savage freakes did fight,
> And ruffling surging seas hath nothing dread,
> By cruel spouses gilt doth lye all dead.

The following passage illustrates Nuce's use of the octosyllable (*T. T.*, 171 a, 1—8, *Oct.* D 1ᵛ) :

> The flasshing fiawes do flappe her face,
> And on her speaking mouth do beate,
> Anone shee sinkes a certayne space,
> Depressed downe with surges great :
> Anone shee fleetes on weltring brim,
> And pattes them of with tender handes
> Through faynting feare then taught to swim
> Approaching death, and fates withstandes.

Nuce's language, as will be seen from these extracts, differs somewhat both from Heywood's and from Studley's. It has fewer Latinisms than Heywood's, and is slightly less colloquial and more archaic than Studley's. Nuce has a partiality for archaic words like 'freake,' and 'make' (meaning 'spouse'), which the other translators neglect, and he employs very largely the prefix y- before the past participle and sometimes before other parts of the verb.

Nuce follows the Latin fairly closely, though he makes no attempt to reproduce the Latin order, as Heywood does in the *Hercules Furens*. He has no additions of original matter of any length, and he does not abridge or alter the choruses, as Neville does. The opening lines of the play may be taken as an example of his method of translation :

> Now that Aurore with glitteryng streames,
> The glading starres from skye doth chase,
> Syr Phœbus pert, with spouting beames,
> From dewy neast doth mount apace :
> And with his cheerefull lookes doth yeeld,
> Unto the world a gladsome day.
>
> *T. T.*, 161 b, 1—6, *Oct.*, B 1.

The Latin is:

> Iam vaga caelo sidera fulgens
> Aurora fugat,
> surgit Titan radiante coma
> mundoque diem reddit clarum

Occasionally, however, Nuce deals with his original much more freely, *e.g.*, *T. T.*, 174a, 21, 22, *Oct.*, D 1ᵛ.

Ne If that I were a meacocke or a slouch
    Each stubborne, clubbish daw would make mee couch.
Sen And whom they hate, with force they overquell,

which represents the Latin

Ne Calcat iacentem vulgus   *Sen* Invisum opprimit

VI.

NEWTON'S *THEBAIS*, AND THE *TENNE TRAGEDIES*.

Thomas Newton, the editor of the 1581 edition of the *Tenne Tragedies*, and the translator of the *Thebais*, was born about 1542, and went to Trinity College, Oxford, which he left for a time to study at Queens' College, Cambridge,[1] though he afterwards returned to his old college at Oxford. About 1583 he became rector of Little Ilford, Essex. He wrote books on historical, medical, and theological subjects, and made several translations from Latin. He translated the *Thebais* in order to make the 1581 volume complete. It is somewhat difficult to judge of his poetical powers from this play, since he undertook it from necessity and not from choice. It is no wonder that the other translators of Seneca had let it alone, for it is not a single complete play, but consists, apparently, of two fragments of plays on the Œdipus legend — the first fragment being an intolerably wearisome dialogue between Œdipus and Antigone, in which Œdipus expresses his determination to die and Antigone dissuades him, whilst the second deals with the strife between the two sons of Œdipus, and Jocasta's efforts to reconcile them.

---

[1] There is no entry in the University records to show that Newton took any degree at Cambridge. According to Anthony à Wood, he became so much renowned, whilst at Cambridge, for his Latin poetry, that " he was numbered by scholars of his time among the most noted poets in that language "

The dialogue between Œdipus and Antigone occupies in Seneca about three hundred and twenty lines, which Newton expands into five hundred, all in the fourteener measure. The weary reader can only wish that Œdipus, who is continually announcing that he means to kill himself by some horrible death, would really put his intentions into practice instead of describing so minutely the tortures he wishes to inflict on himself, or dwelling with such insistence on the crimes he has unwittingly committed, which render him worthy of death in his own eyes.

It was impossible for Newton to make much of such dramatically unpromising material without cutting it down mercilessly, but he does not seem to have felt that his original needed compression. On the contrary, he has a tendency to expand the Latin considerably, and to insert explanatory remarks which, though useful doubtless to the reader unlearned in classical story, scarcely add to the dramatic effect. He is not a slavish translator by any means, his rendering is often very free, but unfortunately he never seems to have noticed that his original needed not expansion but compression. Two examples will illustrate this. Seneca makes Œdipus say :

> quantulum hac egi manu⁹
> non video noxae conscium nostrae diem,
> sed video.

Newton expands this to the following (*T. T.*, 41a, 11—16)

Alas, what litle triffling tricke hath hitherto bene wrought
By these my hands⁹ what feate of worth or maistry have I sought⁹
Indeede, they have me helpt to pull myne eyes out of my head
So that ne Sunne, ne Moone I see, but life in darknesse lead
And though that I can nothing see, yet is my guilt and cryme
Both seene and knowne, and poyncted at, (woe worth the cursed
        tyme).

Again Seneca has (ll. 40—43):

> sequor, sequor, iam parce. sanguineum gerens
> insigne regni Laius rapti furit;
> en ecce, inanes manibus infestis petit
> foditque vultus. nata, genitorem vides?

which Newton expands thus (*T. T.*, 41b, 37—42a, 6):

O Father myne I come, I come, now father ceasse thy rage:
I know (alas) how I abus'd my Fathers hoary age:
Who had to name King Laius: how hee doth fret and frye
To see such lewd disparagement: and none to blame but I.
Wherby the Crowne usurped is, and he by murther slayne
And Bastardly incestuous broode in Kingly throne remayne.
And loe, dost thou not playnly see, how he my panting Ghost
With raking pawes doth hale and pull, which grieves my conscience
    most?
Dost thou not see how he my face bescratcheth tyrant wyse?
Tel mee (my Daughter) hast thou seene Ghostes in such griesly
    guyse?

Newton's language has considerable affinity with that used by Studley. It has a distinctly colloquial character in many places, is less dignified than Heywood's, and prefers native words to Latinisms. A striking example of Newton's employment of colloquialisms may be found in Polynices' speech in Act IV (*T. T.*, 53a, 25—38):

But tell mee whyther shall I go? Assigne mee to some place:
Bylike, you would that brother myne should still with shamelesse
    face
Possesse my stately Pallaces, and reuell in his ruffe,
And I thereat to holde my peace, and not a whit to snuffe,
But like a Countrey Mome to dwell in some poore thatched Cot:
Allow mee poore Exyle such one: I rest content, God wot.
You know, such Noddyes as I am, are woont to make exchaung
Of Kingdomes, for poore thatched Cots, beelike this is not straung.
Yea more: I, matcht now to a Wyfe of noble ligne and race
Shall like a seely Dottipoll liue there in seruile case,
At becke and checke of queenely Wyfe, and like a kitchen drudge
Shall at Adrastus lordly heeles, (my Wyues owne Father) trudge.
From Princely Port to tumble downe into poore seruile state,
Is greatest griefe that may betyde by doome of frouncing fate.

Newton speaks very modestly of his own translation in the letter of dedication to Sir Thomas Henneage which he prefixed to the whole volume. After mentioning Henneage's generosity and love of learning, he goes on to say—

And yet (all this notwithstandinge) well durst I not haue geuen the aduenture to approach your presence, vpon trust of any singularity, that in this Booke hath vnskilfully dropped out of myne owne penne, but that I hoped the perfection of others artificiall workmaship, that haue trauayled herein aswell as my selfe should somewhat couer my nakednesse and purchase my pardon And hard were the dealing, if in payment of a good rounde gubbe of Gold of full wayght and poyse, one poore peece somewhat clypped and lighter then his fellowes may not be foysted in among the rest, and passe in pay for currant coigne. Thens I know to be deliuered with singuler dexterity myne, I confesse to be an vnfledge nestling, vnhable to flye an vnnaturall abortion and an vnperfect Embryon neyther throughlye laboured at Aristophanes and Cleanthes candle, neither yet exactly waighed in Critolaus his precise ballance Yet this dare I saye, I haue deliuered myne Authors meaning with as much perspicuity, as so meane a Scholler, out of so meane a stoare, in so smal a time, and vpon so short a warning was well able to performe

The *Tenne Tragedies* of Seneca appeared in 1581 under Newton's editorship. The title runs thus.—

Seneca His Tenne Tragedies, Translated into Englysh *Mercurij nutrices, horæ* Imprinted at London in Fleetstreete neere vnto Sainete Dunstans church by Thomas Marsh. 1581

The volume is a quarto in eights with the collation A⁴ B—E e⁸ F f³. It opens with a dedicatory epistle by Newton to "the Right Worshipful, Sir Thomas Henneage Knight, Treasurer of Her Maiesties Chamber." This is followed by a list of the Tragedies and the names of their translators. The text occupies 438 pages,[1] and on the last page

---

[1] The foliation begins with the text on B 1 Nos 64, 65 occur twice in the foliation, so that there appear to be only 217 ff instead of 219

there is a motto from Ovid "Omne genus scripti gravitate Tragedia vincit," followed by the colophon.

The plays are arranged in the traditional order, beginning with *Hercules Furens*, and ending with *Hercules Œtæus*.

VII.

METRE.

The metre of these Elizabethan translations is an interesting, but hardly an inspiring, subject. The period in which they were written was the quarter of a century between Surrey and Spenser, when poets were busy practising the lesson of order and regularity in metre, and were not as yet sufficiently masters of their craft to try experiments in it.

The staple metre used by the translators is the fourteener, and most of them handle it with monotonous regularity. The cæsura generally occurs after the fourth foot, and the break in the line is so marked that the printers of the octavo editions regularly make a division there, and print the fourteener in two parts, the first containing four feet and the latter three.[1] Any passage taken at random from Studley's translations shows clearly

---

[1] When, as sometimes happens, the fourth foot ends in the middle of a word, the printers generally divide the word, as in the following example from Studley's *Agamemnon*—

> The ruthfull ruin of our na-
> tyue countrey we beheld

Ag, E5, *T. T.*, 152a, 26.

but occasionally the division takes place after the word, as in

> Now peepes she vp agayn, with drouping
> eyes sonke in her head

Ag., F4, *T. T.*, 15b, 22

51

the danger of flatness and monotony to which such
verse was subject.

> With belowinges, & yellynges lowd,
>   the shores do grunt and grone,
> The craggye clynes, & roryng rockes,
>   do howle in hollow stone.
> The bublyng waters swelles vpreard
>   before the wrastling winde,
> When suddenlye the lowryng lyght
>   of moone is hid and blynde
> The glymsyng staires do go to glade,
>   the surgyng seas are tost
> Euen to the skyes, among the clowdes
>   the lyght of heauen is lost.
>
> More nyghtes in one compacted are,
>   wyth shadow dym and blacke,
> One shade vppon another doth
>   more darknes heape and packe,
> And euery sparke of lyght consumd
>   the waues and skyes do mete,
> The ruflyng wynds range on the seas,
>   through euerye coast they flytt
> They heaue it vy wyth vyolence,
>   ouerturnd from bottom low,
> The westerne wynde flat in the face
>   of easterne wynd doth blow
>
> *Ag.*, D7, *T. T.*, 150a, 4—15.

Heywood and Newton try to vary the extreme
monotony of such verse by frequently making the
main pause in the sense occur elsewhere, so that
the logical and metrical cæsuras may not coincide.
This leads to frequent enjambement, as in the
following passage by Newton:

> Apollo by his Oracle pronounced sentence dyre
> Upon mee being yet vnborne, that I vnto my Syre
> Should beastly parricide commit. and thereupon was I
> Condemned straight by Fathers doome   My Feete were by
>   and by
> Launcde through, & through with yron Pins: hangde was I
>   by the Heeles
> Upon a Tree   my swelling plants the printe thereof yet feeles.
>
> *Theb.*, *T. T.*, 45b, 39—46a, 4.

The versification of Neville's *Œdipus* is more nearly akin to that of the period before Wyatt and Surrey, when the number of syllables and even of feet was of little account to the poet, and accent could be shifted at will. The metrical chaos of the first edition of *Œdipus* has already been illustrated in the extracts given in Chap. III, but even in the revised form in which the play appeared in 1581 such lines occur as—

What colour it wants, or what it hath, to me is like vncertayne
Now is it black, now blue, now red, and euen now agayne
Quight out it is.

T. I, 84a, 5—7

or—

Be sure his lyfe, and death, and all, be quight exempt from mysery
Ere thou do once presume to say this man is blest and happy

T. T., 92b, 32, 33

In the latter example the unaccented syllables of 'mysery' and 'happy' are allowed to constitute a rime.

ANALYSIS OF THE METRE OF THE FLINE TRAGEDIES

The metre used in the non-choric portions of the translations (with the exception of Nuce's *Octavia*) is the fourteen-syllable iambic line, or fourteener, sometimes called septenary. The only exceptions of any length are the following —

Scene between Hecuba and Chorus
Troas, T. I, 99a, 17—100b, 20.
Speech of Andromache to Astyanax.
Troas, T. T, 111b, 12—112a, 20
Soliloquy of Thyestes *Thy*, T. T, 86a, 6—86b, 26
Speech of Achilles *Troas*, T. T., 101b, 19—103a, 21.
Soliloquy of Iole *Herc. Oet*, T. I, 191a, 22—192a, 10

Of these the first three passages are in decasyllabic lines riming alternately, the fourth is in rime royal,

and the fifth in the mixed fourteeners and alexandrines, sometimes known as poulter's measure.
In Nuce's *Octavia* the decasyllabic couplet, and
octosyllabics riming alternately are used instead of
the fourteener throughout the non-choric portions.

In the Choruses the following metres are used :

1 Fourteener   *Hipp* , *T. T.*, 66a, 1—67a, 27
          Medea, *T. T.*, 131b, 13—132b, 26.
          Ag., *T T* , 155a, 19—155b, 40.
          Herc (Œt., *T. T.*, 211 a, 15—212a, 21
     Throughout the Choruses of Neville's *Œdipus*

2. Alexandrine.   *Ag.*, *T T* , 142 a, 10—143a, 8.
          ibid , 147a, 16—148b, 4.

3. Poulter's measure (alternate fourteeners and alexandrines)
          Herc. Œt , *T T* , 204a, 3—205a, 20.

4. Decasyllabic iambic lines, arranged

 (*a*) with alternate rime.

  Throughout the Choruses of Heywood's *Thyestes*, and
  Hercules Furens (except at the close of Act III), and
  Studley's *Medea* (except the passage in fourteeners
  mentioned above)
    Also *Hipp. T. T* , 60a, 8—61b, 22 69b, 16—70a, 23
        Troas, *T T.*, 100b, 21—101b, 18.
        Herc. Œt., *T. T.*, 189b, 29—191a, 21.

 (*b*) in six-line stanzas, riming a b a b c c.
        Hipp , *T T.*, 72b, 1—73a, 12.
  Herc. Œt , *T. T* , 197a, 20—199a, 36, 217a, 23—217b, 5. [1]

 (*c*) in seven-line stanzas, riming a b a b b c c (rime royal)
    Troas, *T T.*, 106b, 1—107b, 16, 116a, 6—117a, 10

5. Octosyllabic iambic lines, riming alternately
        Herc. Fur., *T. T.*, 14a, 1—20
        Troas, *T T* , 113b, 11—26. [2]
    Oct., *T. T* , 169a, 1—171b, 26, 182a, 13—182b, 13.

Occasionally single short lines occur at the end of

---

[1] These lines are preceded by a ten-line stanza in which the
rimes are arranged a b a b b c b c d d.

[2] Here it is printed in long lines of sixteen syllables.

a scene, *e.g Hipp* , *T. T.*, 57 a, 3, 75 a, 24; *Thy.*, *T. T.*, 36 b, 26.

Neville's *Œdipus*, especially in the 1563 edition, offers numerous examples of short unriming lines in the middle of a scene, *c.g.* Act i, l 33.

A few of these remain in the 1581 edition, *c.g.* *T. T.*, 92 b, 10 ; 94 b, 3.

L

VIII.

GRAMMAR.

The inflexions found in these translations of Seneca are, in the main, those common to other early Elizabethan works.

VERBS.

The verbal forms are the most interesting, and among them the following deserve special notice:—

Pres. ind.

2nd pers. sing. The usual form is the normal one in -est, -st, but there are several examples of the Northern form in -s, *e.g.*

Thou *beares* as big and boystrous brawnes as Heicules
Hipp , *T T* , 67 a, 1 1.

O double dealing life, thou *clokes* deceiptful thoughtes in biest
Hipp., T. T., 69 a, 1.

Let not thy griefe be gieater then the sorrow thou *sustaynes.*
Heic Œt , T. T , 195 b, 5.

Thou God that *sits* in Seate on high, and all the world dost guide. *(Fd.,* B 4ᵛ, *T. T.,* 82 b, 6

Thou, that in Lacidœmon *dwelles*, and honorst Castors giace.
Theb., T. T., 43 b, 35.

3rd pers. sing. The forms in -s and -th are used indifferently, *e.g.*

Eubœa that doth rise,
With hauty crest ringes euciywhere, and Caphar rocke likewyse
Deuydeth Hellesponus sea and turnes that side to south.
Herc Œt., T. T., 200 b, 12—14.

As chaunce allots, so falles it out this dome abydeth free.
Theb., T. T , 53 b, 38.

3rd pers. plur In the majority of cases this has the usual uninflected form, *e.g.*

> The ruflyng wynds range on the seas,
>   through euerye coast they flytt
> They heaue it up with vyolence
>
> *Ag* , D 7, *T T* , 150a, 13, 14.

All the translators, however, have examples of the form in -s. In some cases this may be due to the necessities of rime, *e.g*

> I do aduise you to bewaie, bewaie (I say) of kynges,
> (A kyndred in whose cancred hartes olde piyuy grudges *sprynges*)
>
> *Ag* F 2, *T. T* , 154a, 7, 8.

> Hangde was I by ye Heeles
> Upon a Tree my swelling plauts the punite thereof yet *feeles*
>
> *Theb* , *T T.*, 46 a, 3, 4

See also *Theb* , *T T* , 46b, 5, *ib.* 50a, 25, *ib.* 52a, 30; *Herc. Œt., T. T.*, 191a, 25.

There are, however, a considerable number of examples for which no such reason can be given, *e g*.

> What secrets daughter deare
> Unknowen, makes you to look so drouselye?
>
> *Oct* , F2\ *T T.*, 180b, 8, 9.

> And blustring winds and [*T T* of] dauingers depe setts Death
>   before theyr eyes *Œd* , D8\ *T T.*, 91a, 4.

In some cases the form in -s is used when the subject consists of two singular nouns united by 'and', *e g*.

> Lo, both the fruites, that vice and virtue giues
>
> *Herc Œt* , *T T* , 217b, 5.

> And it and heat together makes, great straunge, and ruddy,
>   bumps *Œd* , B1\, *T T.*, 81a, 27

There are a few examples in which 'is' and 'was' are used with plural subjects, *e g*.

> Wherwyth my golden crispen lockes is wonted to be crounde
>
> *Medea*, E 4\, *T T* , 131b, 6

> Such plagues and vengeance is at hande
>
> *Medea*, E 7, *T. T* , 132b, 2.

> . . those Nimphes that wonted was to staye The shyppes
>
> *Medea*, D 1\ *T T* , 127a, 27.

All the translators also offer examples of the use of the form in -th in the 3rd pers. pl., *e.g.*

> Whose songes the woodes hath drawen.
>> *Troas*, B 3, *T. T.*, 101a, 9.

But loe two shynyng Sunnes at once in heauen appereth bryght.
>> *Ag.*, F 2, *T. T*, 154a, 3.

> What sharpe assaultes of ciuell Cupydes flame
> Wyth gyddie hede thus tosseth to and froe,
> Thys bedlem wyght.
>> *Medea*, r 8, *T T*, 136a, 22—24.

> Nor hansome houses pleaseth him.
>> *Hipp.*, *T. T.*, 59a, 11.

Those wordes through all my lims, hath stifnesse spred.
>> *Oct.*, G 2v. *T T.*, 184b, 6.

And clottred lumps of flesh the place doth strow.
>> *Œd*, E 4v. *T. T*, 92b, 9.

The misteries whereof the hearers understandeth not
>> *Theb.*, *T. T.*, 43b, 30.

In some passages forms both in -s and -th are used with a plural subject, *e.g.*

> Some from the highest mowntaynes top, aloofe *beholdeth* all
> Some scale the buyldings hallfe yburnte, and some the ruynous wall,
> Ye [*T T*, yea] some there weire (O mischiefe loe) that for the more despyght,
> The tombe of Hector *sitts* upon, beholders of the sight.
>> *Troas*, F 1, *T. T.*, 117b, 8—11.

or—

> The roring seas *doth* drown their voyce and cares [*T T.*, caryes] their cries awaye.
>> *Ag*, E 1v. *T. T*, 151a, 8.

The 3rd pers. pl. in -n is also found, though rarely, *e g.*

> Except they shed her blood before they gone.
>> *Troas*, A 6, *T. T.*, 97b, 5.

By al my Countrey Gods that bene in Temples closely kept [1563, close I kept]
>> *T T.*, 82b, 35, *Œd.*, B 5v

> .   these Mates ben meetst of all
> For me.
>> *Œd.*, F 2, *T T*, 94b, 14.

Pres. subj.

2nd pers sing. In one passage 'arre' is used for 'be':

> Thou Gods (though fierce and valiant) perforce dost chase, and faire
> Dost ouermatch in length of limmes, though yet but young thou *arre.*
>
> *Hipp.*, *T. T.*, 66 b, 39, 40

Pret. ind.

Weak forms sometimes occur in the preterite of strong verbs, *e.g.*

> Feare *shakte* of rest
> From me.
> *Oct*, F 3v, *T. T*, 181 b, 9, 10
>
> He *shyned* blasing brim
> *Herc Œt*, *T. T*, 199 b, 17

A few archaic or dialectal forms occur, *e g* 'yode' (O. E. eode) for 'went':

> Of mates with hir to sea that *yode*
> *Oct*, D 1v, *T T*, 171 a, 14

'mought' (M. E. mohte, a variant for mihte, mahte, formed perhaps on the analogy of dohte, another pret. present verb) for 'might'

> And for the nones my hawty hart, and Princely courage stout
> I did abate, that humbly thee with teares entreate I *mought*
> *Hipp*, *T T*, 64 d,[1] 31, 32

Other forms now obsolete are flang = flung (*Hipp.*, *T. T.*, 71 b, 36), stack = stuck (*Med.*, F 4v, *T. T.*, 135 a, 1), molt = melted (*Herc. Œt.*, *T. T.*, 199 a, 20, 21).

Past part.

The archaic prefix y- (O E. ge-) is used several times by Studley, only twice by Heywood, three times by Neville, once by Newton, and very fre-

---

[1] In the foliation of the *Tenne Trag*, Nos. 64 and 65 appear twice I have denoted the recto and verso of the latter pair by c and d respectively.

quently by Nuce, who, as has been noticed elsewhere, has a love for archaic forms.

Two examples will suffice.

> Some scale the buyldings halfe ybuinte.
> *Troas*, r 1, *T. T* , 117 b, 9.
> And griesly goast to graue with Torche yborne
> *Oct.*, c 1, *T T.*, 166 a, 6

This y- is sometimes erroneously used with other parts of the verb, *e.g.*

> And steine Erinnis in with deadly steps,
> To Claudius Court, all descit left yleps
> *Oct* , B 4 , *T T* , 165 b, 23, 24.

> Whose roring sownd, and craking noise the lesser woods
> I charmes.   *Œd.*, c 3 , *T. T.*, 85 b, 18.

Weak past participles often omit -ed, if the stem of the verb ends in t or d, *e g.*

> Thy fall hath lift thee higher up
> *Troas*, E 3 , *T. T* , 114 b, 8

> You Aares haue yeld a clattrying noyse
> *Medea*, F 5 , *T. T* , 135 a, 22.

> Dame Iuno hath transport the elves
> *Herc. Œt* , *T T.*, 189 a, 27

There are a few examples in which -ed is omitted, though the stem does not end in t or d. In this case it will generally be found that the word following begins with t or d, *e g.*

> . . . if that among you any are
> Constrayne to shed your streaming teares
> *Herc Œt* , *T T* , 216 a, 14, 15

We sometimes find -n omitted in strong past part., *e g*

> This wayward agony hath take his perht wits away.
> *Herc. Œt.*, *T. T* , 209 b, 1.

> . nowe Lycus loe the grownde
> With groueling face hath smit.
> *Herc. Fur.*, 13, *T. T* , 14 b, 1, 2.

> Which Grekes haue writ in registers
> *Ag* , c 4, *T. T.*, 145 b, 3.

Pret. forms in past part.

Occasionally preterite forms are used as past participles, *e.g*

Or hath the tamer of the worlde and greekes renowne lykewyse,
Forsooke the silent howse

Here Fur , G 1, 2, *T T* , 10 b, 2, 3

I haue shooke the seas. *Here. Œt.. T. T* , 195 b, 15

The braseen buclers being shoke did gyue a clattrying sound
Ag E 6, 152 b, 18

On thee that next olde Arcades in heauen thy seate hast tooke.
Hipp , *T. T* , 66 b, 20.

NOUNS

There are very few plural forms of interest.

Clives (= cliffs)	*Hipp* , *T T*., 59 b, 1
Eyen (eyes)	*Theb* , *T T* , 42 a, 10
Grieves (= griefs)	*Theb* , *T T* , 45 a, 16
Howsen (= houses)	*Here Fur* , I 1, 13 b, 1.
Mischieves (= mischiefs)	*Oct.*, B 2s. *T. T* , 163 a, 26

Clives, grieves, and mischieves show the frequent change of f to v in the plural. Eyen (O. E. eagan) retains the O. E. suffix -n, used to form the plural of weak nouns. Howsen is a new formation, found in other sixteenth-century writers,[1] and still existing dialectally, on the analogy of nouns like eyen and oxen. The plural form in O E. was hus, and in M. E. houses.

ADJECTIVES.

The double comparative is sometimes found, *e.g.* 'worser' (*Hipp.*, T. T., 58 b, 16), and the double superlative, *e.g.* 'most extreamest' (*Ag* , c 2, *T T.*, 144 b, 16). The form 'lenger' (*Œd.*, A 2, *T. T.*, 80 b, 24) for 'longer' represents O E. *lengra*, showing i-umlaut.[2]

---

[1] Cp North *Guevara's Diall of Princes*, 194, a/2 The housen wherin they dwel

[2] Golding's translation of Ovid's *Metamorphoses* furnishes an interesting contemporary parallel to these Senecan translations in grammar and vocabulary. Many of the forms instanced in this chapter are also to be found in Golding, *e g* , 'mought,' *Metamorphoses* vi , 471, 'flang,' viii., 551 , 'molt,' xiv., 487, 'take' as past participle, v., 882 , 'lenger,' vi , 63.

IX.

VOCABULARY.

The vocabulary used in these translations of Seneca is full of interest. It varies to a certain extent according to the idiosyncrasies of the different translators, Heywood having a partiality for Latinisms, Nuce for archaisms of English origin, Studley and Newton for colloquial words and phrases. On the whole, however, there is a general similarity in the language of the plays which make up the *Tenne Tragedies*, and it serves as an excellent example of the diction used between 1559 and 1567 by young men of literary tastes and good education.

Certain words present considerable difficulty, and deserve special notice. Among these may be mentioned the following :—

'Marble' is used repeatedly by Studley as an epithet to be applied to the sea or sky, *e.g. Hipp. T. T.*, 56a, 25, "Whereas the marble Sea doth fleete", *Herc. Œt., T. T.*, 192a, 18, ". . . when marble skies no filthy fog doth dim." Readers of Milton will recall in this connection the 'pure marble air' of *Paradise Lost*, III, 564. The *New Eng. Dict.* explains 'marble' in the line just quoted from Milton, and in a line from Phaer 'marble-facyd seas,' as meaning 'smooth as marble,' and takes no notice of the use of the word in the *Tenne Tragedies*. A study of the passages in which the word is used by Studley and

Heywood[1] leads, however, to a somewhat different conclusion. In *Hipp.*, *T. T.*, 71a, 19, we find "A boasting Bull his marble necke advaunced hye that bare" as the rendering of the Latin "Caerulea taurus colla sublimis gerens," where 'marble' represents the Latin 'caerulea.'

In *Hipp.*, *T. T.*, 73a, 17, "the Monstrous hags of Marble Seas" represent the "monstra caerulei maris" of Seneca.

Herc. Œt, *T. T.*, 193a, 8, has "The northern beare to Marble seas shall stoupe to quench his thyrst" as the rendering of "Ursa pontum sicca caerulum bibet." In Heywood's *Herc Fur.*, c3, *T. T.*, 3a, 8, we find "With marble hors now drawn" representing Seneca's "iam caeruleis evectus equis." Apparently the translator associated the idea of blueness with marble, for in *Hipp*, *T. T.*, 66b, 30, "lucebit Pario marmore clarius" is rendered by—

The Marble blue in quarry pittes of Parius that doth lie,
Beares not so brave a glimsyng glosse as pleasant seemes thy face

If marble be taken as the equivalent of 'caeruleus' = 'azure,' 'dark blue,' the force of the epithet when applied to sea or sky becomes clear, and Studley's predilection for it (he uses it frequently when there is no corresponding Latin adjective at all) becomes easy to understand.

'Aleare.'

O well was I, when as I lived a leare,
Not in the barren balkes of fallow land.
Herc. Œt, *T T*, 190 b, 1, 2.

I spoylde thy father Hercules, this hand, this hand aleare
Hath murdred him. *Herc Œt.*, *T. T*, 203a, 37, 38.

The only example of the word in the *New Eng. Dict.* is the latter one just quoted from *Herc. Œt.* The *New Eng. Dict.* explains "? Fated. ? chance-directed," and suggests as a derivation: "? ad Lat. ālcāris, meaning 'belonging to dice'." This explanation does not hold good for the former passage, of which no notice is taken in the *New Eng. Dict.* There is no corresponding Latin word in either passage—"felix incolui non steriles focos," "Herculem eripuit tibi haec, haec peremit dextra." Both the meaning and the origin of the word are obscure. The *Eng. Dialect Dict.* gives 'aleare' as a provincial word used of waggons to mean 'empty, unladen.'

'Cloyne' = 'steal.'

> . . . for feare least thou alone
> Should cloyne his Scepter from his hand
> *Herc Œt* , *T. T* , 216 b, 15, 16.

'Feltred' = 'matted,' 'tangled.'

> And griesly Plutos filthie feltred denne
> *Oct* , c 2ᵛ. *T T* , 167 a, 33

'Frounced' = 'wrinkled,' 'perverse.'

> And settest out a forhead fayre where frounced mynd doth rest
> *Hipp* , *T. T* , 69 a, 2.
> Thus startyng still with frounced mind she walters to and froe
> *Medea*, D 2, *T. T.*, 127 b, 21

The *New Eng. Dict.* gives no example of the figurative use of 'frounced,' except a nineteenth-century one from Saintsbury in a different sense, though it mentions that 'frounce' is used to mean 'to look angry,' which is not quite the same sense as here. The transition, however, is easy, if such a passage is considered as *Gawaine*, l. 2306, "frounces bothe lyppe and browe."

'Overheel' = 'cover over.'

> . . . the fielde
> That all to spatterd lay with bloud, and bones quight overheelde
> Œd , A 5; T T , 79 b, 21, 22

The *New Eng. Dict.* gives no example of the use of the word as late as the sixteenth century except by Scotch writers.

'Plaunch.'

> Alas, each part of me with guilt is plaunch and overgrowne
> Theb , T T , 44 a, 34.

The *New Eng Dict* gives no example of the use of 'plaunch' as an adjective. It explains the verb 'plaunch' as 'to cover with planks'.

'Royle.'

As a verb, = 'roam' (*cf.* Golding, *Metamorph.*, III, 18)

> Let them in solemne flockes goe royle
> Here Fur , 1 2, T. T., 14 a, 5

As a noun, = 'monster' (?)

> That ugly Royle heere heates him selfe
> Hipp , T T , 71 b, 4.

> These royles, that please to worrey mee
> Medea, G 5, T T , 138 b, 18

The *New Eng. Dict.* gives two substantives under 'roil or royle,' the first meaning 'an inferior or spiritless horse, a draught-horse (of Flemish breed), or a clumsy or stoutly-built female,' and the second meaning 'agitation or stirring up (of water).' Neither of these suits the quotations here given, since that from *Hippolytus* refers to the sea-monster which a few lines before had been described as a bull, and the passage from *Medea* refers to the Furies

Among Heywood's Latinisms the following may be noticed:—

'Frete' or 'freate,' meaning 'sea' or 'flood'[1] (Lat. 'fretum'), *e.g.*

> And freate that twyse with ebbe away dooth slyppe
> And twyse upflowe.   *Herc. Fur.*, D 4, *T. T.*, 6 a, 13, 14.
> And hardened top of frosen freat he troade,
> And sylent sea with banks full dumme about.
>   *Herc Fur*, F 5, *T' T.*, 9 a, 12, 13.
> Thou fearefull freate of fyre .
> O Phlegethon.   *Thy*, *T T*, 39 b, 14, 15.

'Roge,' meaning 'funeral pile' (Lat. 'rogus'), *e.g.*

> And roges for kings, that high on piles we reare.
>   *Troas*, *T. T.*, 100 a, 29.
> What bretherns double tents? or what as many roages also?
>   (Latin   quid totidem rogos?)
>   *Herc. Fur.*, E 3, *T. T.*, 7 a, 19.

'Impery,' meaning 'dominion' (Lat. 'imperium'), *e.g.*

> .   . the auncient note and sygne of impery.
>   *T. T.*, 24 b, 20.

and also meaning a 'command,' *e.g.* "at ease he doothe myne imperies fulfyll" (Lat. "laetus imperia excipit") (*Herc. Fur.*, B 5, *T. T.*, 1 b, 32).

'Stadie,' meaning 'a race-course,' 'stadium,' *e.g.* "Renowned stadies to my youth" (Lat. "celebrata inveni stadia") (*T. T.*, 27 b, 6).

A fuller list of the more unusual words employed in the *Tenne Tragedies* will be found in the Appendix.

---

[1] The *New Eng. Dict.* gives only 'strait' as the meaning of 'frete', but its use here seems to be wider, and to correspond to the use of 'fretum' in Latin poetry to mean not merely 'strait' but 'sea'.

BIBLIOGRAPHY.

I. TEXT

LATIN

Senecae Tragoediae Venetus in Ædibus Aldi et Andreae Soceri
MDXVII

L Annei Senecae Cordubensis Tragoediae Basileae apud Henri-
chum Petri. MDL

L Annei Senecae Cordubensis Tragoediae Apud Seb Gryphium
Lugduni, 1554.

L Annaei Senecae Tragoediae Recensuit et emendavit Fridericus
Leo Berolini, MDCCCLXVIII

L. Annaei Senecae Tragoediae Recensuerunt Rudolphus Peiper
et Gustavus Richter Lipsiae In aedibus B G. Teubneri
MCMII

ENGLISH

HEYWOOD (Jasper) *The sixt tragedie of the most graue and
prudent author Lucius Annens Seneca,* entituled Troas, with
diuers and sundrye addicions to the same. Newly set forth
in Englishe by Iasper Heywood, Student in Oxenforde
London, 1559.

HEYWOOD (Jasper). *The seconde tragedie of Seneca,* entituled
Thyestes, faithfully Englished by I Heywood
London, 1560

HEYWOOD (Jasper). *L A Senecae Tragedia* prima quae inscribitur
Hercules Furens . in anglicum metrum conuersa
. . . per I Heywoodum. London, 1561.

NEVILLE (Alexander). *The Lamentable Tragedie of Œdipus the Sonne of Laius Kyng of Thebes out of Seneca* By Alexander Neuyle   London, 1563

NUCE (Thomas) *The ninth Tragedie of Lucius Annens Seneca,* called Octauia Translated out of Latine into English, by T N. Student in Cambridge.   London [undated].

STUDLEY (John) *The Eyght Tragedie of Seneca* Entituled Agamemnon. Translated out of Latin into English, by Iohn Studley, Student in Trinitie Colledge in Cambridge
                                        London, 1566,

STUDLEY (John) *The seuenth Tragedie of Seneca,* Entituled Medea. Translated out of Latin into English, by Iohn Studley, Student in Trinitie Colledge in Cambridge. London, 1566.

NEWTON (Thomas) [editor]. *Seneca. His Tenne Tragedies,* translated into Englysh.   London, 1581,

SPENSER SOCIETY. Reprint of " *Seneca His Tenne Tragedies* "
                                        Manchester, 1887,

II. CRITICAL AND BIOGRAPHICAL.

BOAS (F S) *Works of Thomas Kyd*   Oxford, 1901.

CHETWOOD. *The British Theatre.* Containing the Lives of the English Dramatic Poets.   London, 1750.

COOPER (C H) *Annals of Cambridge*   Cambridge, 1842-53.

COOPER (C. H and T C) *Athenae Cantabrigienses.*
                                        Cambridge, 1858.

CUNLIFFE (J. W.) *The Influence of Seneca on Elizabethan Tragedy*
                                        London, 1893

FISCHER (Rudolph) *Zur Kunstentwicklung der englischen Tragodie* von ihren Anfangen bis zu Shakespeare.
                                        Strassburg, 1893.

HEYWOOD (James) and WRIGHT *Cambridge University Transactions.*   London, 1854

JOCKERS (Ernst) *Die englischen Seneca — Uebersetzer des 16 Jahrhunderts*   Strassburg, 1909.

BIBLIOGRAPHY

KALUZA (M) (Trans A C Dunstan) *Short History of English Versification.* London, 1911.

MILLER, (F J) *The Tragedies of Seneca* translated into English verse Introduced by an Essay on the influence of the tragedies of Seneca upon Early English drama by John Matthews Manly Chicago, 1907.

SAINTSBURY (G.) *A History of English Prosody* London, 1906.

SCHELLING (F. E) *Elizabethan Drama* Boston and New York, 1908.

SCHIPPER (J.) *Neuenglische Metrik* Bonn, 1888.

SMITH (G. C. Moore) *Plays performed in Cambridge Colleges before 1585* (Article in *Fasciculus J W Clark dicatus*) Privately printed, Cambridge.

STEPHEN (Leslie) and LEE (Sidney) *Dictionary of National Biography.* Articles on Heywood, Neville, Newton, Nuce, and Studley London, 1885—1900

STRYPE (John) *Life and Acts of M. Parker* London, 1711. *Life and Acts of J. Whitgift* London, 1718.

SYMONDS (J. A) *Shakespeare's Predecessors in the English Drama.* Revised edition London, 1900

WARD (A. W.) *History of English Dramatic Literature to the Death of Queen Anne.* 2nd ed. London, 1899.

WARD (A W.) and WALLER (A R) *Cambridge History of English Literature,* Vols V and VI Cambridge, 1910

WARTON (T.) *History of English Poetry* London, 1774—81. Edited by Hazlitt (W C) London, 1871

WOOD (Anthony à) *Athenae Oxonienses* Ed P Bliss London, 1813—20

APPENDIX

A list of the more unusual words to be found in the *Tenne Tragedies* of 1581.

This list does not claim to furnish a complete glossary. The references are to the foliation of the 1581 edition. The derivations given are for the most part based on information found in the *New English Dictionary* as far as it has appeared.

AARE (O. F. aire, L. ara), altar   186 b

ABANDON (causative use of vb.), banish, cause to abandon   58 b
"Nor Taurus mount whose hoary and frosty face
With numming cold abandons all inhabitors the place"

AGRISE (O. E. agrisan), terrify   66 b, 189

ALDER (northern form of 'older'), former   64 b, 134 b

ALEARE (see pp. 63, 64), etymology and meaning uncertain. According to *N. E. D.* not found elsewhere   190 b, 203

APPEACHE (represents an earlier *anpeche, prob. A. F. form of O. F. empechier), accuse   65 d

APPOSE (var. of oppose), confront with hard questions   43 b

ASSOYLE (pres. ind. and subj. of O. F. asoldre), solve   79 b

ATTACH (O. F. atachier), accuse   165 b

BASNET (O. F. bassinet), steel head-piece   51

BATTAYLOUS (O. F. batailleus), warlike   175

BEAR THE BELL, take the first place   48 b, 65 c, 166 b

BEFROUNCED (be + frounce = wrinkle), ruffled   214 b   *N. E. D.* gives no other example of the word

BERAY (be + ray, aphetic form of array), disfigure   181, 183

BESTAD (be + stad and O. N. staddr), beset.   10 b, 160

BETHWACT   *N. E. D.* gives only bethwack = pelt, thrash   53 b   The meaning here seems to be 'covered' "a soyle bethwact with vines"

BLEAKISH (bleak + ish), rather pale   67   The only example in *N. E. D.* of this use of the word

BLOCKAM   Etymology and meaning uncertain.   Not mentioned in *N. E. D.*
"And some at least to blockam Feaste to bryng"   198

BOALNE (prob. from O. E. bolgen, past part. of bolgan), swollen   196 b, 200

70

BOBLING (onomat), babbling   156 b

BOOD (incorrect use of *bood*, pret of *bide*, in the infinitive), abide, 147

BOUGH (onomat), bud   155 b

BRASELL (prob Span brasil), hard wood, 188 b

BRAY (O F braire), give forth   *N E D* adds ' with a cry,' which does
   not suit 64, l 29
   "Or els among the baulmy flowres out braying famous [? samours]
   sweete"
   Cf 56, ll 12, 3
                              " where Zephirus most milde
                        Out brayes his baumy breath so sweete "

BRIM (O E breme), bright   180, 192, 199 b

BUFFE (O F buffe), buffalo, wild ox   56 b

BUGGE (prob Weslh bwg), hobgoblin   201 b, 206 b

BUGLE (O F bugle), buffalo, wild ox   56 b

BUM (deriv uncertain), strike   64 b, 183 b

BUSKLE (freq of *busk*), prepare, shake   189, 192, 212

BYLBOWBLADES (from Bilbao in Spain, famous for its swords), sharp
   swords   143 b

CHOP (prob var of chap=buy), exchange   161

CLEAZE (plur of clea, clee, which represents the O E nom clea, cléo,
   as claw represents the oblique cases, clawe, etc), claws, 74 b,
   188 b, 206 b

CLERESOME (O F cler+some), bright   3   Not in *N E D*

CLOTTER (freq of clot), clot   69, 92 b

CLUBBISH (club+ish), clownish   174

CLYP (O E clyppan), embrace   29 b

COLL (O F col), embrace   29 b, 51

CON THANKS (O E thanc cunnan), offer thanks   47 b

CONQUEROUS (conquer+ous), victorious   180

CORSEY (syncopated form of coresive — corrosive) grievance   193, 206

COUNTERMURE (F contremurer), fortify with an additional wall   64 b

COUNTERPAYSE (O F contrepeser), counterbalance   67 b

COYLE, subs (deriv uncertain), tumult   43, 189 b, 52 b, 183 b

COYLE, vb (deriv uncertain), beat   156 b

CRAKE (var of crack), boast   As subs 141, 151, as vb 166 b

CRANKE (deriv uncertain), vigorous   201 b

CRISPEN (var of crisp, crisped), curled   62, 64 b, 131 b, 204   This form
   of the word is not mentioned in *N E D*

DANKISH, danky (deriv of *dank*), somewhat dank   167, 106 b

DARRAYGNE (O F deraisnier), contest, challenge   46 b

71

F

APPENDIX.

DIMILAUNCE (F demie lance), light horseman armed with short lance 152

DINGTHRYFIE (ding + thrift), spendthrift   198

DISPONSED (Lat desponsare), betrothed   152 b   *N. E D* gives only *despoused*, for which this may be a printer's error, though it appears in both editions of the text, or it may be a new formation from the Latin

DISKUMPE (Lat dis rumpere), break up   177 b

DISTAYN (O F desteindre), defile   42 b

DORRE (prob O N dár), mockery   85

DOTTIPOLL (dote + poll), blockhead   53

DOWSE (prob ononiat though it may be connected with douse = strike), plunge   74   *N E D* gives no example as early as this, and states that the word appears c 1600

DRAKE (O E draca), meteor   66

DROSEL (deriv uncertain), slut   168 b   *N E D* gives the word only as subs, but on f 145 b it is used as an adjective
' This drosel sluggish ringleader "

EARNEFULLY (adv from earneful, var of yearnful, from yearn), anxiously, sorrowfully   191 b

EASTERLING (from easter [adj] + ling, prob after Dutch oosterling), native of the east   188 b, 211

EFTSONES, immediately, repeatedly   34, 105

EMPEACH (Fr empêcher), hinder   43 b

ENGRAVE (in + grave), entomb   20

ENMIOUS (O F enemieux), hostile   15 b

ENTENTIVE (O F ententif), attentive   194

ENTREATANCE (entreat + ance), entreaty   64 c

FADGL (deriv uncertain), fit   166 b

FEERE (O E gefera), companion, spouse   43 b, etc

FELTRED (O F feltrer), matted   167

FISK (prob frequent of O E fýsan), move briskly   192 b

FITTERS (deriv uncertain), fragments   73 b

FLAWE (prob O E *flagu, corresp to Swed flaga), squall   69, 167

FLIMFLAM (prob onomat), idle   137 b

FLINGBRAYNE (fling + brain), foolish   47   Not as adj in *N E D*

FLUSH (prob onomat), flutter   60 b

FONDLING (fond = foolish + ling), fool   194, 198

FORLORNDE (use of *forlorn* as trans vb , meaning 'lament')   141 b

FORSIOW (O E for-slawian), delay   214

FREAKE (O E freca), man   162 b, etc

FREMMD (O E fremede), stranger   48 b

72

FRETE (Lat fretum), strait, sea, flood   6, 9, 37 b, 39 b

FROUNCED (O F froncier), wrinkled, perverse   69

FRUMP (vb), mock   177 b

FULGENT (Lat fulgentem), glittering   27 b, 66

FUSSTEN TUMIS (fustian – coarse cloth, fig inflated language), display of anger   153 b

GAINER (compar of O N gegn), straighter, more direct   57

GARBOYLE (O F garbouil), tumult   47 b, 48

GARGELL, gargle, adj (O F gargouille), monstrous   60 b, 123 b, 138 b

GAITEN TREE (O E gate treow), dogwood   64 b

GIRD (deriv uncertain), thrust   71 b

GLADE (prob Scand), setting (of sun or stars)   66, 161 b, 198

GLEDE (O E gléd), light, fire   68 b, 71, etc

GLOWM, GLOWN (deriv uncertain), frown, lower, 192 b, 210, 217

GLUMMY (glum + y), dark   71, 188 b, etc

GLY (deriv uncertain), look asquint   188 b

GNOFFF (cf E Fris gnuffig = rough), churl   198

GOAR (from gore [subs] = blood), cover with blood   188 b

GOBBET (O F gobet), fragment, piece of flesh   72, 75

GREETE (O E gréotan), weep   207 b

GRUTCH (O F groucier), murmur at   177 b

GUB (O F gobe, goube), lump, clot   72, 175 b, etc

GYDON (O F guidon), flag   49

HAPPY, vb (from happy, adj), make happy   115

HAWSING (O E hals), embracing   65 c

HAYTING (hait, a word of encouragement to horses), crying 'hait'   167 b
    N E D gives no example of its use as adj

HEGGE (var of hag), evil spirit   204 b

HELLICKE (O E hel-lic), infernal   67 b, 73

HELLY (hell + y), internal   5 b, 18

HENT (O E hentan), seize   43

HOY (prob M Dutch hoei), sloop   190

HUGGER MUGGER (deriv uncertain), secret   58

HUGY (huge + y), huge   35, 64 b, etc

IMP (O E impa), child, scion   64 d, 209 b, etc

IMPERY, emperie (O F emperie, assimilated in the form impery to Lat imperium), (1) dominion, 2, 24 b, 29 b, (2) command, behest, 1 b
    This latter use is said to be rare by N E D which gives no other example   •

JAUNCE (deriv uncertain), make prance   199

JET (O F jeter), strut, swagger   194 b, 198 b

JOTTING (prob onomat), jogging. 56b, 72.

JUMPF, adv (from jump, vb), exactly 183

KARRAYNE, adj (var of carrion, O Norm F. caroine), death-like, corrupt 190, 211 b

KAYSAR (Lat Caesar), emperor 201 b

KERERENFS (a var not mentioned in *N E D* of carerie, var of career) 63 b

KILL (var of kiln), funeral pyre
>   "and thus the forrest wyde
>   Doth make the Kill [for Hercules' burning]" 213, 1 8
>   " When up he stept on Oeta mount and gazed on his Kill "
>   *ibid* 1 13

N E D gives no example of this use, though the transition to it from the ordinary meaning 'furnace, oven' is easy

KNAPPE (onomat), break in pieces 19, 212 b

KNARRIE (M E knarie), knotty 64 b, 202 b, 213

LABEL (O F label), fillet, ribbon 64 d, 66

LACTUSE (var. of lettuce, Lat lactuca), sea-weed 71

LARME (F larme), tear 216 Not in *N E D*

LAUNCH (O Norm F launcher), pierce 168

LAUNCING (O F lancier), darting forward 149

LEAME (O E léoma), flash, ray 193 b, etc

LEEFF, subs (O E léof), love, husband. 167

LIMERE (O F liemier), leash-hound, blood-hound 56 b

LINNE (O E linnan), cease 44, 201, 210 b

LITH (O E lithe), calm, still 70 b

LUMPF (and lower), vb (onomat), look unpleasant 150

LUSKISH (vb lusk = skulk), sluggish 57 b

MAI'D (aphetic form of amayed = dismayed), dismayed 103 b

MANKINDE, adj masculine, virago-like 156 b

MARBLE, adj (see pp 62, 63) 3 56, 58 b, 61, 61, 67 b, 68 b, 71, 71 b, 73, 192, 193, 193 b, 216, 200 b

MEACOCKE, meycocke (deriv uncertain), coward 45, 151, 174

MELL (O F meller, mesler), interfere 54 b

MENY (O F mesnie), retinue 155

MICHING, myche (prob O F muchier), skulking. 69, 193 b

MISER (Lat miser), wretch [without idea of avarice]. 22, 28, etc

MOARY (var of *moory*, from *moor*), marshy 196 b, 210 In 'hoary moary frost,' 133 b, it has probably no force of its own, and is used only for the jingle

MOME (deriv uncertain), blockhead   150b, 198

MOYSTED (from *moist*), moistened   36b

MUCKY (N E muk), dirty   190

NOCK, vb (from nock, subs = notch), provide bow or arrows with notch   147b, 213

NOTE (ne + wot), know not   25

NOWNE (from *own*, by mistaken division of *myn own, thyn own*, and used afterwards with *her, your*, etc), own   171b

NOY, NOIANCE (aphetic forms of *annoy, annoyance*)   206b, 72b

OBIT RYTES (L obitus), funeral rites   74b, 149b

OBTAYNE (in Lat sense of *occupy, possess*)   61

OVERDIGHT (over + dight), cover over   162b

OUERHEEL (O E oter-helian), cover over   79b, 84b   N E D gives none but Scotch examples after 1200

OUERQUEL (over + quell), perish, be overcome   152   N E D gives examples only of the transitive use of the verb

OUERTHWART (over + O N thveit), across   151

PALT (var of pelt), strike with repeated blows   191b

PARBRAKE, perbrake (compound of brake - vomit), vomit   69b, 159b

PASH (onomat), break in pieces   50, 191b, 206

PATCH (possibly from fool's patched coat, or perhaps from Ital pazzo), fool   174, 177

PAYSE, subs (O F peis), weight   21b, 64

PAYSE, vb (O F peser), weigh, balance   17b, 162b

PIPLING (dimin of pipe), whistle   70b, 134b

PLACKET (L placet), expression of assent or sanction   189b

PLUMP (deriv uncertain), troop, flock   81

POYNT (aphetic form of appoint), appoint   22b, 32b

PRIG (deriv uncertain), steal   64

PRINCOCKS (deriv uncertain), coxcomb   165b

PYKES, pass the (F passer les piques), run the gauntlet   45

QUAIL (deriv uncertain), impair, destroy   44b, 15b

QUARELLE (O F. quarel), arrow   55b

QUARIE (var of quarelle), arrow   190b

QUAYNT (O F cointier), acquaint   64

QUEACHY (queach = thicket, + y), forming dense grove or thicket   48,

QUELL (O E cwellan), kill   41b, 69

APPENDIX

RACE (var of rase, raze), scratch   72

RACK (deriv uncertain, prob Scand), mass of cloud   60b, 196

RAHATE (var of rate), scold   53b

RAMPIRE (O F rampar, change of vowel in second syllable unexplained), rampart   4b, 64b

RAMPYRE, rampei (O F remparer), fortify   172b

RASCAL, adj (O F rascaille), inferior   56, 211b

RAY, subs (prob aphetic form of array, or perhaps direct from O Norm F *rei, O F roi), array   48b, 71b   .

RAY, vb, soil   92b

REAVE (apparently due to confusion of reave = rob with rive), cleave

RECTOR (Lat rector), ruler   11b

RECULE (O F reculer), retire, drive back   149b, 190

REGALL, subs (F regal), feast   64

REPRIVE (var of reprove), reject   163

RETCHLES, reachlesse (O E recceléas), careless, heedless   70, 74b

REXE (deriv uncertain), merry-making   156

RIG, ryg (deriv uncertain), (1) ransack, rifle   92b   (2) romp   57b

ROGE (L rogus), funeral pyre   7, 99, 100   The only example in N E D dates from the latter part of the seventeenth century

ROORE (M Du roer), disturbance   212b   N E D gives the word only in the phrase in, on, or upon a roore

ROYLE, subs (see p 65), ? monster   71b, 138b

ROYLE, vb (deriv uncertain), roam   11

ROYST (from roister, F rustie), swagger   63

RUFFE (deriv uncertain), fury   59

RUNDEL (var of roundel), circle   175, 176

RYVENED (confusion of riven and rived), cloven   170, 178   No mention of this form in N E. D

SAFETINESSE (safety + ness), safety
           "the daungerous quick Sand
  Shall promisse Ships with safetinesse upon the shold to land"   65
  Not in N E D

SANGUE (F sang), blood
           "Descended of the royall Sangue"   46
  N. E D gives only "sang royal," with no example of the inversion of the phrase

SHERYNG (O E scieran), clearing [water]   149b, 162b

SHITTEL (M E schityl), rash, headlong   58b, 62

SHIVE (M E schive, schife), splinter   64b, 21

SHOG (var of shock), shake, jog   167b, 189

76

SLABBY (slab = mire, + y), wet, slimy   71, 189

SMOT (verbal subs from smite), stroke   160 b

SPANG (O E gespong), ornament   198 b

SPELL (? O N spolı), splinter   72

SPLAY (aphetic form of display), display   102

SPRITISH (sprite + ish), ghostly   170 b

SPYRE (L spira re), blow   151

STADIE (L stadium), race-course   27 b

STEAMING (O E stéman), glaring   188 b, 201

STIVING (? O F estiver), hasty   148 b

STOUPE (Icel stölpı), post   68

SWALLOWE, swolue (M E swolwe, gult, whirlpool   70 b, 74

SWINCKE (O E swincan)   The usual meaning of 'toil' is not apparent
in this passage
            "In olde Assaracks goblets gylt they
            swincke and swill the wyne"   156

TAT (deriv uncertain), let fall   No example of this use in *N L D*
            "The fainting horse for sodayne paine from back his
            burden tats"   80 b

TAW (O E tawian), flog   68

THIRL (O E thyrlian), pierce   56 b, 208

THIRL, thril, thurl (deriv uncertain), hurl   56 b, 48 b, 192

THRATLING (var of throttle), choking   152

UGSOME, ougsome (O N uggr + some), frightful   192 b

UNGRUBBED (un + grub – dig), not dug   173

UNPAYSED (un + payse = weigh), unbalanced   191 b

UNREKY (un + reky = moist), unmoistened   207 b

UNWAYNED (un + wayn = bring), not advanced   191 b

URE (O F cure), operation, use   123, 141 b

VER (O F ver, Lat ver), spring   66

VIRAGO (Lat virago), woman of great strength and courage [without de-
preciatory force, here applied to Diana]   56 b

WALME, wawme (O E wælm), wave, ripple   145, 149, 195 b

WALTER (freq of walt = roll), roll, welter   62 b, 81, etc

WAMBLING (M E wamlen), rumbling, heaving   133, 190 b

WANNY (wan + y), pale   66 b, 191

WAROUS (ware + ous), full of waves. 43 b

WAYMENT (O F waimenter, guaimenter), lament 48 b

WAYNDE (O N vegna), brought 50 b, 142 b

WHIST, whisht, whusht, 1 b (whist, interject, onomat), be silent, 30 b, 7, 18 b

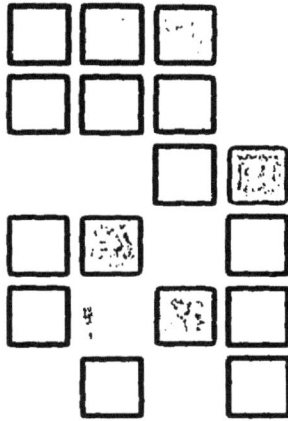

Milton Keynes UK
Ingram Content Group UK Ltd.
UKHW012015010224
437136UK00005B/131

9 781020 489105